Why Psychotherapy?

WHY PSYCHOTHERAPY?

Nini Herman

Drawings by Josef Herman

'an association in which the free development of each
is the condition of the free development of all'

Free Association Books / London / 1987

First published in Great Britain in 1987 by
Free Association Books
26 Freegrove Road
London N7 9RQ

Reprinted in 1991

British Library Cataloguing in Publication Data

Herman, Nini
    Why psychotherapy
    1. Psychotherapy
    I. Title
    616.89'14   RC480

ISBN 0 946960 71 2 hb
ISBN 0 946960 72 0 pb

Printed in Great Britain by Billing and Sons Ltd, Worcester

Contents

Author's Note: Concerning gender, I have used the masculine throughout since I find that 'he or she' interrupts the flow of thought and plays havoc with the main rhythm aimed at in sentence structure.

Preface

As a young family doctor in the National Health Service, I began to recognize that I was sadly unequipped to help many of my patients. They suffered from something other than the range of illnesses we students had been taught about. Trapped in hopelessness, depression, insomnia and other symptoms where physical examination generally drew a blank, their malaise was, in fact, neurosis. That Freud had mapped this shadowland in terms of cause and effect, and had forged a remedy for these ills, our lecturers in psychiatry had not so much as mentioned once.

To rectify my professional impotence, and to explore the problems that dogged my personal life as well, which I have written of elsewhere (Herman, 1985), I enrolled in the training to become a psychotherapist. A ten-year apprenticeship included psychiatric 'jobs', one in a teaching hospital: a distressing, painful sentence. That our patients there were suffering from some emotional disorder, a broken sequence of events in their personal history which could be understood and consequently rectified to a significant degree with psychotherapeutic skills, was almost totally ignored. The task in hand of understanding patients like these in depth or of initiating a therapeutic partnership within whose dialogue they might discover their own true selves so as to heal and start to reach for the rewards of self-fulfilment – the skill and time this would require were hardly on the horizon. Instead, each 'case' was taken over by a so-called 'expert' who would set out to 'treat' the patient. Highly dubious medication, much of it known to be harmful in terms of causing addiction and other serious side effects, was nearly all that was on offer. Chronicity and suicide rates continued to rise steadily.

Nor were there signposts in this no man's land as to where future doctors, nurses, police, social workers, patients and their families, could be directed to find help. Small wonder that medical students, with only rare exceptions, came to hate psychiatry and to find it very boring. It became their pet aversion, as long ago it had been mine.

Sanity is an element which we can now identify, as is argued in these pages. At this time in our history, human survival may depend on our courage to acknowledge this self-evident fact and to foster the insight. The reasons for opposition to such a point of view are examined here. Life affirmation must conscript us to oppose the cynicism which insists on 'treating' people and to offer them instead the dignity to heal themselves and thereby to facilitate a restoration of our era, since the two go hand in hand. Once we learn, by deepening insight, to recognize sanity, we are at last in a position to unveil its subversion wherever it exists; for sanity enables us to learn from experience, a capacity we – tragically – have otherwise to forfeit. Acceptance of these hard-won truths is growing from a grassroots level which surely merits our support against the cruel prevailing cutbacks and professional attitude of laissez-faire as it predominates in what is called psychiatry in Britain today.

Introduction:
Approaching a Predicament

It would, I think, be true to say that for over two decades I had really loved my work as a family doctor in the National Health Service, the contact with so many people from entirely different backgrounds and a role which offered me a place in the community, with which I could become involved in various satisfying ways. It seemed improbable, at first, that anyone could ask for more. Yet, as the working years rolled by it began to puzzle me that nine tenths of my time was in fact occupied by some quarter of the patients whose names stood on my 'list'. Their folders grew and grew and grew. Other patients I might see once or maybe twice a year, many still less frequently. But, as always, it took time to obtain these basic bearings, and, looking back on it today, I can see that I only tumbled to these matters after working two assistantships and after sufficient time to settle into a practice of my own. Sooner or later, nonetheless, I must have tuned into a question: what was the meaning of these signals which were alerting me every single working day to the existence of a problem that the medical curriculum of my wartime student years had apparently failed to touch upon?

My patients, with their bulging folders, brought me various complaints. Investigations, as a rule, tended to be negative. There might be a diagnosis which looked respectable enough, but yet could hardly justify such frequent

1

attendances. Provided I was able to find the time to listen in to what these sufferers tried to tell me, with sufficient interest, despite fatigue and irritation, I recognized that here were plaintiffs who were bringing their lifelong grievances to me. Sometimes, these would focus on a variety of symptoms with a tendency to blame them on their relationships, or perhaps the lack of them; at other times, the focus would be on their employers or their fellow employees, or, not uncommonly, on installations in the home that were always breaking down and that no-one seemed to fix, at least not to their satisfaction. These patients were like children in distress whom nobody could pacify.

These troubled and perplexing people began to draw my interest. They seemed to get under my skin like a welcome irritation, with all the paradox implied. I was like the Pied Piper of Hamelin; my growing interest drew them in, and their proportion on my list began perceptibly to grow, as did my anxiety, which was rooted in a new admission on my part that I clearly lacked the skill to bring about some improvement in such obvious misery.

By the early 1960s, after almost a decade, the drug companies proclaimed that they were coming to the rescue. Psychotropic remedies began to flow onto the market to fill a range of rainbow shelves in every dispensary. Tranquillizers, stimulants, sleeping capsules and much more rolled in ever growing numbers off a new production line, in a climate of euphoria. The commercial travellers, known as representatives of the drug companies, haunted doctors' surgeries at closing time and enthused: here was an end to mental illness. It was uphill work to challenge their optimism, despite one's persistent apprehension that these excellent intentions were paving the secret path to hell. And in less than a decade, papers started to appear in the medical journals claiming that certain remedies were causing drug dependency which might prove harder to break than existing addictions to morphine or heroin.

By the time that this cat had escaped from the bag, I was already working as a psychotherapist. In a weekly group I ran in a teaching hospital, I soon discovered that my efforts had now to be concentrated on helping a number of these addicts break their dependence on a list of tranquillizers that their Doctors had prescribed. Only then could we begin to try and take a closer look at their real anxieties rooted in deeper conflicts. Nonetheless, this project required considerable fortitude, because the patients' withdrawal symptoms could be painfully severe and also very frightening.

My decision to train as a psychotherapist had come about for two good reasons. There was firstly my real interest in these unhappy plaintiffs of whose condition I was clearly in total ignorance, although as students we had 'done' three months of psychiatry. Secondly, I recognized that my own mental health, if I was honest with myself, stood in need of close attention; obvious disarray prevailed in my personal life.

By the time that I resigned from my own general practice to embark on my course, family doctors in the UK were already issuing something like 20 million items of prescription for tranquillizers, anti-depressants, pep pills and sleeping drugs in any single year (Sally O'Brien, 1986). A woman in the West Midlands was reported in the *Sunday Times* to have recently returned 12,400 unwanted anti-depressant tablets to her doctor's surgery. She had evidently hoarded these regular repeat prescriptions over several years for a dark and rainy day. In this case, there was a happy outcome, which nonetheless revealed the tip of an enormous iceberg. Now, at the time of writing, suicide by overdosing, so-called parasuicide, is an epidemic, growing by some 10 per cent a year. According to the Registrar General's Hospital In-Patient Enquiry of 1977, over a quarter of a million people a year at that time were being admitted to our hospitals with drug overdoses. A follow-up enquiry has suggested that something like one fifth of these unhappy people will actually kill themselves over the next 20 years, and it has been estimated that 75 per cent of these self-poisoners are using drugs obtained from a doctor, of which a proportion are issued by psychiatrists. A number of our population are hanging on from day to day on the tacit understanding that where all else fails they can always turn to death by prescription, painlessly. The psychoanalyst Betty Joseph has written of this state of mind as a 'chuntering' with death, meaning a state of mind where death is always an option kept in a person's mind (Joseph, 1982). Once I had been alerted to this macabre syndrome, its prevalence, however frightening as a reflection of a sick society, could no longer be denied.

Such was the perplexing background, general and personal, against which I 'went back to school', when I was well into my forties. To study these phenomena, to be of help to these plaintiffs, and to set my own house in order, meant that I had to acquire an entirely new skill. I also had to undergo a personal analysis seeing that it was a case of 'physician, heal yourself' before you try your hand on others or, more correctly put, your own mind. Family doctors by tradition are inclined to see themselves in the role of exorcist. They may believe that they have shared a prerogative as soul-healers with the Shaman and the priest since the days of letting blood. That there is, in fact, a skill both in listening and in replying, of infinite complexity and dazzling sophistication, has frequently not dawned on them. That the painstaking researches of Freud and his followers, over a century, have slowly opened up vistas in depth psychology quite as far-reaching as those wrought by the microscope in infectious diseases, has so far failed to percolate through to the medical curriculum. Psychiatry, as we shall see, has in essence retained a nineteenth century attitude, if not a mediaeval one, whilst acquiring a thin veneer of hit-and-miss technology by chemical brinkmanship. In no other branch of medicine would such hocus pocus be permitted these pseudo-rational displays.

What precisely is it that the psychiatrist is up against? Or, for that matter what afflicts the so-called psychiatric patient, the person who has broken down, or is no longer functioning as society prescribes, who is no longer performing by expectation or by rote but has a baffling absence of any bodily default known to science? Of course the full hue and cry following a chemical explanation echoes loud and clear through the world's laboratories. The brain is placed in a test tube but the mind flies away to mock the white-coated ranks of those blinkered scientists with peals of sardonic laughter or at other times with tears. And still our plaintiff is complaining at his doctor's surgery or to the psychiatrist. What is he, or she, more often, actually complaining of? The colour has drained out of life. Morning and evening, spring and summer, Monday, Sunday, all look bleary, vaguely threatening and grey. Meanings which the day once carried now hang indistinct and blurred. Satisfaction, joy in others, pleasure that was found in work, leisure, family and friends, have slipped to irritation now. Every conversation seems to turn into an argument, until there is a gradual drift to a chilly no man's land where virtual isolation reigns. And yet, so imperceptibly has this mind slide taken place, past frontiers that were never crossed, landmarks that passed unrecognized, that none of this can be defined.

That this sequence of events is comprehensible in terms of a life history, if we can only tune into it, still continues by and large to escape psychiatry. For once that discipline is pushed beyond the realm of nerves and brain, of physical structures, towards the territory of the mind, there is only Jargonese, which is waved around like incense to ward off evil spirits and to keep us whole and safe from harm. 'Retardation'; 'thought disorders'; 'hallucinations'; 'delusions'; these terms throw virtually no light on why a human life has stalled at this particular moment, any more than 'engine failure' would satisfy investigators into a car or plane crash. The reality is that a pair of people, a patient and a chosen guide, are facing no lesser task than to unpick a lifelong tangle, a learning process which has run into a maze of deep confusions, of atrophied or stunted feelings, of faulty self-representations, which may even have affected the sexual identity, so that there is no medication, no chemical panacea which we could reasonably expect to answer as a substitute for the slow and arduous task of providing that asylum of the close relationship known as psychotherapy. How the tangle comes about we shall be looking at. For the moment, let us point to a condition known as 'maternal reverie'. We tend rather to take for granted that a mother, after giving birth, is entirely preoccupied with her infant. It seems that she monitors the baby's fluctuating states of mind with a degree of subtlety, a range of sensitivity, in the first weeks and months of life, which no other relationship in later life can hope to match, although our yearning will persist to recreate its ambience in the love life of our adult years. With the maternal reverie, the mother strives to contain the confusions and anxieties, which include the fear of dying, that her infant will communicate; she takes them into her own mind with her sharpened intuition, filters them of their distress and returns them to the infant in a far less threatening form, so that the infantile mind can begin to digest them. As this process continues round the clock of days and nights, running into weeks and months, being phased out gradually, the infant slowly learns to confront the components of emotional experience increasingly on his own. The baby will discover, bit by bit, what he is able to contain and digest unaided and what help (without which he feels overwhelmed or threatened with disintegration), is needed. This maternal 'There, there, there', to put it into its simplest terms, familiar to all of us, helps to lay our foundations for mental health and sanity. It is a relationship of container to contained, one which we urgently return to at times of illness or of stress; but even when our life runs well, it is an aptitude we value in every close relationship since lack of it is experienced as a major

deprivation, which it is painful to endure in the daily wear and tear.

But what happens to the infant where this provision fails in relation to his needs? In my own experience, many doctors who are drawn into psychiatry look to that discipline as to a Containing mother for their own anxieties. This attraction is unconscious, something which, in other words, they may well not be aware of. The deeper 'reasoning' runs like this: if psychiatry can help those whose mind seems to be stalling, then psychiatry must be what I myself am looking for. If Symptoms of a disordered mind can be classified and named, then by that magic they can be conjured away and 'got rid of' or, at any rate, controlled. This assumption, which is based on primitive magical thinking, can transform a department of psychiatry into the front line in a battle, where some shout forwards and others back. The department can, to be honest, be a very frightening place where it may prove quite difficult to distinguish very clearly between patients and the staff.

A number of psychiatrists soon see matters in this light and so decide to train as psychotherapists. In the course of training they are required to undergo a personal analysis which will last for many years. In other words, they will submit to a minute scrutiny of the workings of their minds; the deepest conflicts and malfunctions of one mind will be explored by the mind of another who was analysed before. To put it simply, the trainee will look for a containing mother however late in his own life, to permit anxieties which were denied or repressed in his early infancy and subsequently in his childhood, to surface now, belatedly, so that they may be understood and gradually modified. This healing process will in time help him to be less afraid of deep anxieties in others, and also help him to develop his own Capacity for maternal reverie towards those who may seek his help.

At the time of writing, psychotherapeutic skills make up rather less than 10 per cent of the total personnel hours offered by National Health psychiatry in the UK. This means that patients seeking help in understanding themselves must either go without or turn to the private sector. In the London area, at a very rough guess, two to four thousand people make this choice every year. In other parts of the country, possibilities of help are very few and far between for lack of adequate provision. We will come on to the implications of these facts presently.

The individual's state of mind, its harmony or its disorder, its capacity for containment or its tendency to spill out and poison the environment with hatred or with paranoia, is of paramount importance, not only to that individual or the closer family, but in terms of wider ripples coursing through society and eventually the world. There was a time when religion served its community with a yardstick and a guideline. It encouraged the believer to monitor his inner life and set his inner house in order. The truth of our inner life, our inner world, and our motivation, was always held before our eyes. Our relationship to God, to our transcendental yearnings and our highest ideals were not allowed to sink from sight into a morass of greed and mindless power politics without, at least, a fleeting comment. How far the practice proved effective for mental health lies outside our present scope. Society's disintegration at its present night-rider speed is a highly complex issue. Nonetheless, its microcosm must remain the state of mind of the human individual. This and this alone can serve as a bastion against chaos and an antidote to violence. Where we fail to invest in this primary resource, no other measures will avail. Whether we travel to the moon or tunnel underneath the sea, all these projects will be fruitless and ultimately doomed by our self destructive drives if we fail to pay attention to the child in distress, raging within the adult and wanting to be pacified. The adult, asked what ails him or her, will be unlikely to offer more than an angry outburst or perhaps a flood of tears. I still remember the young woman in a mental hospital, newly come into my care, who wept for practically an hour in response to that question. Perhaps these pages will assist an approach to answer how the likes of you and I may either help ourselves or others to find the answer to this question in patient, guided exploration, gradually, step by step.

My objections to psychiatry, as taught and practised today, could of course be argued from a wide variety of platforms. I have here chosen a largely experiential one. Even the concepts which are presented here were selected in as far as they became a part of me. Such a learning process is, to some degree, idiosyncratic. (However, the bibliography at the end of this book indicates my original sources.) The book should not be read as an attack on my colleagues in psychiatry, except insofar as I ask them the question: what would we say to a builder who consistently ignored the advances of a century?

When I was a medical student, four whole decades ago, the psychiatric 'back wards' where chronic patients were housed, were like scenes from Dante's *Inferno*. Sadly, some such wards still exist. Electroconvulsive therapy, used for severe depression and melancholia, was given 'neat', meaning without anaesthesia or the muscle relaxants which have since come into use. What one was witnessing was an epileptic fit induced by an electric current applied at the temples to the brain. Fractures were not uncommon, including sometimes to the spine. I felt anger and dismay at this human interaction, which at a deep, unconscious level seemed suspect and negative. A maintenance engineer once claimed, as the story goes, that a certain ECT machine had in fact not worked for months, although the clinical findings drew no attention to the fact. In my heart I admonished psychiatrists known to use the procedure extensively and kept my patients well away from them and from their methods. Years later, one such eminence addressed the entire staff in an asylum where I worked. He began by telling us that he had been a junior doctor in this very hospital. At the time there was little he could do for his patients other than keep them sedated with bromide and paraldehyde and play endless games of tennis with the superintendent, which he was obliged to lose in the interests of promotion. There were tears in his eyes as he spoke of the suffering he had been unable to relieve until one day, lo and behold, this magic box called ECT had come along, offering the longed-for manna to his sufferers. Yet, as I now looked more closely at his fine, ravaged face, I could read very clearly a history of melancholia and personal suffering in a deeply caring man.

None of us should forget that madness is a scourge which makes harrowing demands. We can all be tempted to convert our own outrage, fear and pain at this cruel phenomenon into one-upmanship, by resorting to impressive jargon, to pretend omniscience, which, of course, includes myself. If psychiatry today is far from perfect, let us still pay tribute to those who daily go down to this wild sea in little snips, at risk to their own sanity and for so little reward or recognition from the rest. It is out of respect for them, as for those in their care, that I would wish to see things better and at least good enough.

Lastly, let me clarify that the technique for looking at a person's past, the history-taking outlined in Chapter One, is one I forged to suit myself in busy hospital conditions, where time is always at a premium. It is a hybrid that I found useful under those circumstances. It must not be confused with its more distant relative, the more searching assessment which may be used to explore a patient's suitability for long, intensive individual treatment.

1

Every Story Has a Meaning

M edical students need to learn how to take a history. Illness does not as a rule fall out of a clear, blue sky. It is a failure which evolves, although we may neglect the signs and carry on being quite unaware that anything may be amiss for an alarming length of time. For in the daily wear and tear we drive our bodies quite relentlessly. We do the same thing with our minds, so badly are we out of kilter with these two mainstays of our life.

A sound physician will become something of a Sherlock Holmes. The way in which an illness starts will tell him a great deal about its nature, its true direction, and the possibilities of its eventual outcome: that is, its total meaning in the patient's life. He will base his treatment on quite subtle aspects of these findings, if, as a doctor, he is something more than one more whizzkid of the modern age: in that case, he would simply name the illness like a deity and conjure up a remedy when, hey presto, he has wrought a cure. This technocratic approach attempts to wave an omnipotent magic wand and subdue an incubus. All concerned will be euphoric. The patient need not scrutinize any of the deeper warnings, mindless habits or his way of life, which is in essence that of an absentee from the scene of his own self. The surface has been briefly ruffled but the depths at least are not disturbed, that is, until the next blow comes along. Doctor and patient, in this case, are not a healing team. Their relationship is one of a father to a child where the latter is absolved from all responsibility. The requirement is merely that the 'child' takes his case away, imbibes the latest wonder drug as he has been told to do and reports back at intervals until one day he is discharged: end of story. Excellent.

Sometimes, however, more attention will be paid to the patient's personal words. History-taking talks about a person in distress, deep in conflict and uncertainties. Here we have the privilege of listening to a dialogue, to a deepening exchange between two participants collaborating at the task of elucidating a meaning. Where true physicians are at work, we discern a process which initiates a healing programme rooted in true partnership. Physicians of that stature were among my teachers in the wartime north of England. They have become a rarity nowadays. But, recently, things have turned full circle and we find a slowly growing interest in the whole person once again. It is slipping in through the side door of a new holistic medicine, if a little furtively.

Psychiatry does, of course, record a patient's history, but here, histories are taken with patriarchal zeal to give 'this business' a name, followed by the latest pills, which will chase 'it all' away. In more disturbing circumstances, the patient may be taken in and slotted into a regime which seems designed for imbeciles, and carries one end in view— to soothe a 'nasty episode' and ease the patient back to work with a minimum of fuss. Here, psychiatry aids and abets a world that wants a brand of nice, tidy outcomes which need not raise those awkward questions concerning the human psyche: that individual as a whole.

Yet looked at from a healthier angle, mental illness represents a potential growing point. This may apply even to its more dramatic forms such as psychotic episodes. Here, a loosening has occurred within an inner state of mind, resembling a jigsaw puzzle; badly assembled pieces have somehow been locked into disarray. Now, some change of circumstance or of inner alignment has acted as a catalyst and suddenly flung the components of this stalemate far apart; the hope is that the pieces may now be reassembled in a manner that would give life a meaning, provided there is outside help. Histories should be seen as an approach to the individual's deepest psychic structure and unconscious motivation. But psychiatric history-taking as it is practised today glances at the exterior instead of penetrating to the depths; it attempts to know about, but fails to understand; it remedies and exorcises but invariably fails to change the matrix gradually by intervening in the total scene, enriching the entire soil, as all true gardeners will do before they sow a single seed.

Knowledge and understanding ideally constitute a team. But this is often not the case. Candidates who bash their way through so-called higher education with its plethora of exams are certainly in a position to intimidate their fellow human beings but may have no inkling of wisdom or true understanding; these depend on mental depth and a searching curiosity which cleverness will often lack, for all its superficial glitter. When our sufferer at last confronts this professed expert known as a psychiatrist, he will as yet be unaware that it is understanding and not knowledge that is thirsted for, a deeper understanding that he needs, has probably never known and has been deprived of cruelly; or that it is this crucial lack which underlies the whole malaise – all the bother and travail and shadow boxing of his life.

The object, then, of history-taking will be to move gradually towards a growing understanding of where and how the trouble lies within the landscape of the whole. Furthermore, this grasp will be shared in due course, as is the responsibility for planning any of the steps which we call treatment. Where the end in view is seen as labels hung hastily on a superficial reading of mere outer signs, this, by default, becomes a tomb in which all hope for genuine growth and true development is laid to rest, a miscarriage in the course of which honest opportunity has been shabbily subverted.

A subversive history will not have been taken carelessly.
The contrary may be the case. Pages and pages will contain
full details of the patient's life, only to occupy the reader's
mind in an exhausting, fruitless way. Yet as one gets towards
the end, a weary realization will dawn that nothing in the way
of insight has been established or achieved; we will feel
devastated by this self-defeating exercise. Yet the stakes, we
have to remember, are no less than a human life.

To illustrate my attack on the 'subversive' history I will
now give extracts from four long sheets (with slight omissions
and some minor changes for confidentiality). This patient
was referred to me with this history in his file to ask me
whether I believed that psychotherapy might help.

Past Medical History:

Complains of: Double vision. Prescribed specs but
double vision persists. 10 years living
with woman. Break-up sexual reasons.
Pressures causing double vision. Now
she has moved back to help with small
son and patient has moved out leaving
them together. She had said she didn't
love him any more. He wanted to go on
as before. No arguments. Could cope
with son if eyes are OK. Intends to keep
son. X (the woman) does not want the
child. Lived previously with 2 other girls.
Thought with X it was for ever.
Feelings of depression. Occasional anger
with himself. V. hard coping because of
sight.
Appetite normal
0 weight loss
0 suicidal tendencies
0 sleeping. Awake until 3/4 am.

Drug History:	Anti-depressants. Doesn't feel the same person since taking them. Needs sleeping pills.
Family History:	M 60 years. No psych. problems. F dead at age 54, when patient was 23. Close to M not F. Reasonable marriage between Ps. Bro 40 years. Alive and well. Sister 39. Alive and well. Patient 34. Brother 30. Depression, attempted suicide. Childhood happy.
School:	Left 15 years. Plumbing. Truant occasionally. Relates with teacher OK.
Work:	Likes his work. Friends at work.
Past Medical History:	0 accidents 0 illnesses 0 psychiatric instability
Mood:	Flat now since he's moved out. Can cope. Lived alone before. Staying with M in M's flat. M is sympathetic.
Leisure activities:	Smokes. Listens to Records. Reads, except for eyes. Smokes 10-12 a day. Alcohol: restarted after problems. Anxiety as eyes 'become funny'. Dry mouth because of pills. Very hard to be jolly.
Summary:	34 year old plumber who c.o. double vision after breakdown of relationship with his 'wife' after 10 years. Break gradual with growing tension over past 3 years. Unexpected. Cannot accept this. 7 year old son. Wants custody but cannot cope because of eyes.

This is not a history which was selected specially but was the first to come to hand. It is in every respect a typical example of psychiatry at work today. We assume that it was taken either by a 'clerking' student or a houseman, possibly, who was doing his first job. By a beginner certainly, but by a beginner who is faithful to a style which he was taught and whose approach to his patient is therefore classical. In any event, the histories which some consultants take are practically identical although a small minority achieve a true, perceptive style which conveys a human being in his own, unique distress so that our feelings are engaged in the first paragraph.

Of course it is important that we teach a methodology. Nothing as important as drug addiction should be missed, or something as significant as suicidal thoughts omitted. But here the methodology has been imposed from *outside*. We have a record here which is devoid of inner links or any sign of empathy, and will never lead us to the essential interior since it lacks intuition and has killed perceptiveness.

However, something has taken place. We feel a deadness and despair. After reading through this tract we will probably feel overwhelmed with hopelessness, as well as anger, a sense of futility, because we have ended up with the history-taker's state of mind: as hopeless, blank and confused as was the sufferer's in this case. So what, we ask, has taken place? What has been the interaction at this sorry interview? We may reasonably assume that the sufferer has pushed, or 'projected', as we say, all his deadpan hopelessness and arrogant hostility into this young psychiatrist who was simply overwhelmed, hardly surprisingly, but who was entirely unaware of this excruciating process because he was never taught to observe and monitor his own state of mind, which must be the history-taker's most sensitive instrument.

Drilled in external format to the exclusion of his inmost feelings as a guideline, our poor young colleague has become a soldier in a battlefield of the most uneven chances. Numb and frozen stiff with fear which has got to be repressed, since his teachers never taught him how terrifying mental illness and its strategies can be, he has blindly and numbly stumbled to the bitter end. And we have been dumb witnesses to one more bravado act repeated through an endless day in which psychiatrists become the passive receptacles or unwilling containers for their patients' massive backlog of infantile psychic pain which they will never learn about throughout their training in its present form.

Medical students become doctors who become psychiatrists who have never even heard of this crucial term above or experienced it as their own. Here is a phenomenon which colours every known illness and determines its outcome in diverse and subtle ways, which decrees the nature of much psychiatric illness and the outlook in each case, while psychiatrists take shelter behind their ECT machines or their psycho-pharmacology. Their predicament resembles the familiar picture of the forces of law and order in South African townships, when they put on a show of strength in their armoured vehicles as the rocks begin to fly, obliterating their vision every time one hits the windscreen. Fear or rampant fantasy that there will never be a prospect of amelioration keep the sides too far apart from any genuine dialogue.

The interview here has ended with each protagonist in a wretched state of mind. Our history-taker has withdrawn, quite considerably shaken, but with no time to lick his wounds before the very next affray. The wretched sufferer has, meantime, taken himself away in the belligerent confusion in which he recently arrived, feeling, if anything, more hopeless, and clutching his assorted pills as his one and only lifeline in an uncomprehending world. His appointment to consult a nebulous entity labelled 'psychotherapist' has not been made by consensus, but come to him decreed from above for no reason better than the history-taker's ardent wish, of which he may be unaware, that he may

never again be exposed to this shattered man who spreads
his affliction like the plague.

I will presently return to this sorry case and give certain
extracts from the psychotherapist's report. But first of all let
me enlarge on the objections I have raised concerning such
history-taking, for it could readily be claimed that all that I
am doing here is showing a young doctor up. How I wish that
this were a case of youthful inexperience which could be
remedied over time, instead of such a serious matter as
mental health lost by default. Like a senile patriarch,
psychiatry stays deaf and blind to the true nature of the mind,
refusing to acknowledge that Freud proclaimed its deeper
laws of clear-cut cause and effect a full century ago. Now,
only popular demand can initiate some change so that we
might inform ourselves and discover how to take responsibility in stages for our darker states of mind.

If this kind of history-taking fails to such a serious degree,
is there an alternative based on genuine understanding of the
mind's development to guide us in an interview? The end
in sight, after all, is to help a sufferer to gain a clearer picture
of him or herself, in slow stages, through patience and col-
laboration.

If you were to draw a railway line, you would put the
stations in, clearly, with some emphasis. Stations matter, after
all. There our journeys start and end. Stations offer choices
and alternatives; we either travel on or change direction, as
the case may be. We may change our minds and travel back
to whence we came, if we suddenly feel terrified, or lost or
homesick. Where mental illness is concerned, people do
this all the time. The question which concerns us when we
take a history is how far back the traveller has returned and
just how far he might have travelled forward before such a
retreat began.

Every deeper change of mind and of purpose has its roots
in those layers of the mind which are known as the
unconscious. Decisions are not taken, as a rule, where

mental illness is concerned, for clear reasons to do with what we call the conscious mind. If this were the case, our history-taking would be a very much more simple task. Here, we are confronted with unconscious conflicts in the mind in someone we have never met or even heard of previously; we have a mere hour, or even less, to start to make a little sense of the darkness which prevails in a human being's life. It is a daunting undertaking that demands application of a deeper methodology: an inner, not an outer one based on a clear understanding of the mind's development, that line we travel on from birth, through childhood, on to adolescence and from there to maturity. The task demands furthermore, that we are not on the defensive, but open, both in heart and mind, to this other in distress who has come to seek our help. He may have travelled a long distance, in many senses of that word, to brace himself to take this step out of the lonely desert regions which have been his habitat for longer than he may remember. He may well be terrified at this step that he has taken towards the acknowledgement that he may require help from another human being, something which he has quite possibly denied throughout his life. He may expect to be dismissed with a haughty or a hostile quip. He may do everything he can to subvert this interview, this frightening opportunity. All these matters we must know about and bear quietly in mind, as we take the meeting step by step, working in his interest and equally in our own, since we must, of course, protect our own equilibrium, the machinery of our sanity. We have responsibility for the mental equilibrium of both partners to this opening dialogue.

Returning to our patient now, the man whose notes we quoted from, how far back might he have travelled from the little that we know? He went back all the way to 'Mum'. But from these notes we cannot tell just how far that really was. From these notes, we cannot glean details of the actual distance which this unhappy man 'regressed', as psy-chotherapists say. It may have been a very short one. He may have never left this 'mum'. He may have remained an infant at the breast, for all we know, just going through the motions of trotting off to school, doing an apprenticeship and setting up a new home, in which he lived on as an infant, or at least in a state of abject mental dependency, dark grievances and frustrations, in combat with a hostile world which seemingly expected him to work and fend for himself instead of taking care of him. If anything, the notes suggest that there was nothing much amiss in the life of this man until the mother of his child suddenly walked out on him. A bolt hit him from the blue and affected both his eyes, so that he could no longer cope with his responsibilities, but went back home to live with Mum.

Now this sounds none too plausible. So let us take a closer look from our 'dynamic' point of view, that is, exploring the realm of the energies and drives in the deep layers of the mind: the conflicts of our inner world. Personal development – in terms of the human mind – has stations all along the line. They are crucial in human life. To assess them properly, in any given case, may require years of work in the course of psychotherapy. But in one hour or thereabouts (all the time we may be given in a busy hospital for an initial interview), all that we can hope to glean for diagnostic purposes is a very basic groundplan in these developmental terms. Very often we would need two or three such interviews at convenient intervals to obtain a clearer picture on which to base a diagnosis, which in turn helps us to decide on the best approach to treatment. Yet we may not get these. The workload under which we stagger in the National Health Service is unrealistic and absurd. We carry it at the cost of only doing half a job. We know this is the case and feel discouraged, depressed and exhausted far too frequently. A rich society like ours ought not to economize on such serious human matters which affect the individual and thereby his family which in turn must affect the larger group, in widening circles, spreading despair and disarray which may in turn breed violence and encourage addictions to either alcohol or drugs. This laissez-faire attitude is new to medicine in my experience; it has developed over almost half a century. And since psychiatry reflects prevailing social attitudes with abundant accuracy, genuine changes within the field are even further discouraged, in a mean and tawdry climate where the 'forces of the market' take priority over human wellbeing. Ought we then to be surprised at the obstacles we meet if we orientate ourselves towards laws of cause and effect, instead of being satisfied with the surface of appearances?

But let us return to our history-taking. In psychiatry, we are confronted with a mind in a vacuum. There is no railway line and there are no stations. Students become doctors, who will specialize in turn to become psychiatrists; these psychiatrists see their subject, the mind, as a sort of moonscape desert without meaning, place or time. Or, where some sequence of events, some kind of 'train' is acknowledged, we find no driver, no guard, no passenger, no one; only empty compartments, all along. We have a ghost train in a ghostly land. It is enough to drive one mad (assuming that one is still sane), perusing several histories of this kind in one afternoon.

What precisely does the allegory of the train and the stations of the mind mean seen in terms of human life? Initially, we will of course have to restrict ourselves, keep curiosity in check to wait and see what we are told, just what our patient will select from the plethora of his life; where he keeps us in the dark, we must not forget that he may be largely in the dark as well. Rather than admit this fact, which he may find frightening, he could start making stories up, quite unwittingly of course. For example, we would become suspicious where someone who seems quite ill and significantly out of touch, will insist, as so often happens, 'my childhood was a happy one'.

The notes that we have quoted from imply that our unhappy man appeared to be close to 'Mum'. But that may mean a thousand things, according to the state of mind in which our sufferer arrives. Nonetheless, we can assume that in one so seriously adrift, we are not referring to a closeness where boundaries will be healthy or intact. We will keep a watchful eye for further clues along the line (if we are able to discern them, even now, at second hand), with regard to the transactions between that infant and that mother, several decades ago. Our task is easier since the transactions may be going on, unchanged, to this day, although the infant has become a man, to all appearances. Here will be a state of mind in which we are able to discern how this man relates to us in the here and now.

At station number one we are principally concerned, not with our patient of today, but with the baby who was born. To speak vaguely of siblings, as do these notes, who are 'aged 30 or 40' is palpably ridiculous. Were they aged two, or three or four when our sufferer was born? Did he enjoy the privilege of being the oldest for a while, to be cruelly dethroned, or the youngest, possibly, with everything this might imply? How quickly did he get pushed out when the next baby came along? Was he ready for that blow? Can we locate any clue that the infant he was then had successfully laid down enough ego strength so that when the momentous hour struck, he could deal with his immense frustration, his invidious sense of loss, and go on making healthy growth, despite this abject dislocation? Was his mother 'good enough' to use Winnicott's term (which no-one has yet improved upon)? Of course, our sufferer does not 'know'. But he may answer questions like this: 'Did Mum, when you were small, have time for you? Did you two play together much and laugh and sing and have some fun? Was she a cuddly sort of mum'? If she slowly comes across as a semi-absentee, perpetually preoccupied, in the grip of sombre moods, and obsessed with the urge to maintain a sparkling home, we will keep an open mind; she may have been disturbed, with everything this could imply for her infant's start in life. A mother who is sick in mind cannot serve as a container in the way we have described. What is worse, she may need to use her infant as a container, to relieve her own anxieties, and to lay his fragile mind to waste with all manner of intrusive projections of her own. The infant cannot defend himself against this subtle mind-abuse except by resorting to the most far-reaching strategies, known as primitive defences, which may cripple his own mind in ways we shall be looking at. Even cuddles, we should note, can be pathological, can spell out possessiveness and a confusion of all boundaries, which is far removed from love and which cannot let that infant grow into a separate entity.

Here we should remind ourselves that the answers to the questions we ask an individual may well not take us very far, or may prove misleading in the end, since they belong to an 'outer' rather than our 'inner' method. The answers we are looking for will reach us in a different form, perhaps unsolicited. Provided we are sensitive to the disturbance created in the depth of our responses, the hang-ups and resentments belonging to his infant past, will start to hit us as projections long before the hour is up. All we really need to do is to offer ourselves as that longed-for container to initiate a flow of the innermost disorder which will, in very many instances, happen more quickly than we bargained for.

Let us now return to birth, which we called station number one for our present purposes. This is not identical, we need to remind ourselves, with the so-called 'positions' which will concern us in Chapter 3; the 'positions' belong to depth psychology as conceptualized by Mrs Klein. For our first assessment, we will need to apply a simpler, more direct approach, so that we can obtain our inner bearings, where time is at a premium. The stations we will scrutinize are something of an artefact from which the more dynamic ones, which will be called 'The positions' can be gradually inferred, that is to say by an observer who is conversant with the longhand as with the shorthand method: a well-trained psychotherapist.

Say, for example, a builder asks a customer about the condition of a roof. He will not ask about the slates, the state of timbers or the gutters: he will simply say: 'Does the rain come in at times?' Or, 'Did you notice any dark patches, up above your bed?' In the same way, we will have to ask our sufferer general questions. With the stations which concern us fixed firmly in our mind, we will slant our observations to those areas which we know to be our nearest point for inference, at the same time aware that they are heuristical devices used for these purposes.

Having obtained certain clues about the health or otherwise of the individual's early family life, we turn our attention to the second station on the line, one which tends to stand out clearly in most people's memory; that is, starting school. This is the first time, after all, that a child finds himself standing on his own two feet among strangers. What was that experience like? The message which filters through to us may suggest it was 'OK', it may be shrugged off as a purely irrelevant life event in an ocean of the same, or we may be told kindly to just get lost and stop intruding. We may be informed that school was a better place than home, an opportunity to chat to friends; friends is something we would like to know about. Do we have a loner here? Was he hated? Did he hate everyone who came in sight? And what about authority? Were the teachers pretty nice, or dreadful, or a bit of both? Did he feel that they were on his side, some of them, at any rate, or against him generally? Was the world against him or for him, looking back to then? Standing in the teacher's shoes, during this interview, are we treated with suspicion? Are we told, reading between the lines, to mind our own business, or do we feel some measure of being accepted as a friend, even if with mixed feelings?

If we link the information we are slowly gathering, to the language of our feelings, a picture will begin to form in the depths of our own mind. From these snippets of rough clay, working rather like a sculptor, we will model a portrait, changing and emphasizing, adding here, paring off there, to build up a likeness gradually. Of course, we may wish to know about matters like school exams, but our primary concern will be with inner states of mind as they pinpoint inner strength or weakness. We need to look at the cracks and see just how serious they are. Are they only in the plaster, or in the actual elevations? Are the foundations strong enough or on the verge of caving in? We must be aware that despite the appearances of success (such as a good university degree and evidence of intellectual ability), a personality may be precarious in the extreme, may be so fragile as to cause considerable concern. From past experience we know that, whatever happens, we must never be misled by the outer accomplishments, the status or the wealth that our sufferer may have achieved. There may be an adult part of a personality which has learnt a certain trick of functioning well, in isolation from the rest. The rest may be a shrinking child. The rest may be quite terrified, no more than a babe-in-arms, while this pretender or 'false self', as psychotherapists call it, is up and out there, in the reeling world, wheeling and dealing with a great big name, fooling everyone in sight. Only we must not be fooled. Only we may not betray the confidence of that small child who has come to us for help. We must tactfully convey that we have seen through the disguise and picked up the cry for help, while transmitting our respect for such an act of courage; for nothing less than courage is required on the part of those who are prepared to end a lifelong game of hide-and-seek, which we all like to play to the end of our days – for we are all like ostriches who put our heads in the sand of the unexamined life.

To return to our enquiry, or rather to our work as it takes shape beneath our hands, our station number three might be the point when the individual first left home. A sensitive landmark, this; we need the details of how and when it was accomplished, and if, in reality, it ever really was. Did our sufferer stay at home until the very day he married? In that case had he met a woman to found a new family, or had he merely slipped across from one warm bed into the next? Had he run away from home, from a family situation which had blocked all paths to further growth, where parents could not tolerate, as is so frequently the case, a child's own struggle to become a clear and separate entity, one whose ideas would be his own, and would, if different from theirs, come under fierce attack? In such a family a child who threatens to become a separate concern, instead of a compliant member of a strict clan, may be hounded mercilessly even to the brink of madness, even beyond, to suicide, as R.D. Laing and his colleagues (Laing and Esterson, 1970) have so very clearly shown.

But there again, our individual may have tackled this momentous step of setting out from hearth and home in positive and hopeful ways; he may have tried his wings more gradually while remaining in close touch. In such a case, we might be dealing with less traumatic difficulties, instead of with those serious cracks of diagnostic gravity. In any event, we want to know how the whole transition went. Were there panic states and bouts of despairing loneliness papered over by wild and precarious socializing? Did he smoke or drink to excess, or develop curious attitudes to food, either eating too little or too much, by way of an attempt to deal with inner emptiness, with the bleak sensations of an inner void? Did he have some dim awareness of a big black hole, a yawning maw that terrified him and became filled in with wild distractions and various manic states of mind?

Along this line of enquiry, we skirt the addictions, in their obvious or some hidden form, like fierce attachment to a single friend in a morbid or possessive way. Were there experiments with drugs? Did he phantasize an overdose every time that things went wrong? Alcohol and drugs are part of a dark picture of this kind; a puzzled parent may see them as nothing more annoying than an aspect of 'keeping bad company', but they are rather more than this. Here, we are in a landscape of the so-called perversions, as we gradually slip towards a sexual history. In many cases, this will just emerge quite readily, by itself, provided we wait quietly, our fingers toying with the clay.

In those 'outside' histories where so much violence is done to the inner music of a life, sex is often noted in cold isolation from the rest and everything that went before. Accordingly, we come across: '1st sexual intercourse at 18'. Reading this, we recognize that we are in a vacuum. No stepping stones have led us to this fragment on the written page. The capacity for intimacy starts at station number one, almost from the hour of birth. It will find expression in the cosy, loving, bedtime ritual of hugs and cuddles and true warmth, all the playfulness of love, where love alone can instil the sense of life affirmation in which the experience of being wanted for oneself – ontological security – can gradually take root and grow. We have to bear in mind that later on, sexual life, including marriage, can quite easily be an expression not of love but of infantile dependency (which frequently runs very close to hatred and pathological control of the partner in effect). Nothing that we stumble on in the kind of history which pursues an inner trail should come to us as a wild surprise. Instead, the story should unfold, as will the structure of a plant once its genus becomes known to the horticultural eye and hand of long experience.

Let us move to the question of satisfaction found in work, station four or five, perhaps. There we may find the little boy whose daddy taught him how to use a hammer and nails, to mend a fuse, or fix a gate, or ride a bike, so that he approaches adolescence with quite a number of ideas on how he hopes to use his hands or brain, or both, out there in the wider world. That world he senses as a friend. He anticipates that it will be eager for the contributions he will make out of the fullness of his love. But when a father is aloof, cold and hostile, or where he is an absentee, either in reality or in the heart of that boy's mother, then the boy may cast around in meaningless, half-hearted ways, only to withdraw at each frustration or slight obstacle from a world he experiences as hostile, as an enemy.

How can such a little boy ever identify with the life tasks of a man? How can he dream of marrying a girl one day, just as Daddy had once found and married Mummy? How can he think of a farm that he might work, a plane he might fly, a car he might fix, or books to study, bridges to build, wells to dig in distant lands thirsting for this kind of skill? How can he dream of fatherhood, of a partner who will bear their children beneath the roof which he has set above their heads, to keep his family safe and warm? Instead, we will expect to hear that this boy, who was deprived of a father's steadying love, has lost this old, protective instinct which is built into fatherhood, only to drift from pillar to post until work grinds to a halt, more for inner than for outer reasons.

Much the same applies to girls. Where mother was initially the centre of the home and world, where she was first a big, warm lap and then a presence in a kitchen, well suffused with lovely smells, where she often welcomes help; if, furthermore, she engaged in creative interests, outside in the wider world with enthusiasm as a woman in her own right, here was a model which would prove meaningful for the girl. With this she could identify, as a source of inspiration, or differ from in various ways. This she could rebel against, if at times she felt the need, and then return to, presently, to sift and sort her inmost quest for personhood and identity.

No father or mother can, obviously, guarantee a child plain sailing into mental health. We must never forget that the constitution of each infant, his unique disposition will play their own decisive part. But where troubles come along, in the course of a life, parents who were 'good enough', will more probably have laid foundations on which the growing child can later build, even in more serious cases, where it may take years of work to reach back to this *terra firma* after carefully dismantling the debris of catastrophe.

It may sound easy, put like this. But even the 'inner' history our intuitions piece together can encounter hidden traps which will mislead us, particularly with regard to an adequate assessment of the hidden strength of the self-destructive impulse, meaning deflected aggression. In that event we may find that the power of the death instinct gains ascendancy over the drive of life and love, where the two have become defused to a worrying extent.

A young woman whom I saw illustrates this point. She had been busy setting up an academic career in the human sciences. A part of her had forged ahead to take the challenge in her stride. However, she suffered badly from lengthening bouts of depression which increasingly disabled her and were grave setbacks to her hopes and plans. Now she sat there facing me, complaining long and bitterly about her mother who had never shown her, she was convinced, sufficient warmth and sympathy. She overwhelmed me with examples of her mother's coldness and neglect, as someone in continuous pain. On the other hand, we found ourselves returning now and then from these dark tunnels to the light of a very different scene. There we met a mother who felt very different, who had once felt close and cuddly and even something of a friend. This mother had, it seemed, enjoyed growing roses very much. When the patient finally finished her list of grievances, after maybe half an hour, I asked her, just off the cuff, whether she had ever liked gardening by any chance. Her heavy and unhappy face, with its persecuted look, began to brighten and light up. She said that as long as she could remember, she had loved growing flowers and had always hoped to have a garden of her own.

Possibly, I tried too hard to locate some signs of hope. I certainly did not pick up any hostile undertones or competitive nuances in these life-affirming words, and so arrived at the conclusion that psychotherapeutic work should eventually reach back to that 'good', early mother, for all her daughter's bitterness. Later, however, it became clear that I had, in fact, overlooked the seriousness of deeper factors in these depressions which recurred with such malign persistency. In our subsequent discussions, the girl wished to have no truck with individual psychotherapy, because it meant paying for it. To have to pay meant, to her, that she was not loved for herself, as is so commonly the case. Thus, she chose to join a group. I sensed that she was basically frightened to commit herself to the closer one-to-one relationship and hoped that she might manage this after some period in a group, where she would begin to learn something of self-scrutiny. She had to wait to join the group, as I explained, for several weeks. I saw her once halfway through this waiting period as agreed, and everything seemed well enough. It seemed to me that she was coping with the frustrations of the delay in a reasonable state of mind. Then two weeks later I was told that she had been hospitalized with a massive overdose. She was still in hospital eight weeks after the event and did not want to know about individual psychotherapy, although anti-depressants and ECT had, predictably, not worked. Her self-destructive impulses had made a clean sweep of it, for she had handed in the job on which her whole career rested, quite securely, at the time.

Was I taken by surprise at this turn of events? The answer is yes and no, for reasons we will look at now. First of all, there was the issue that any help she would receive had to be on her own terms, namely that she should have it free. It was a point of principle, she announced angrily. Nor was she open to my comments that having to pay did not mean that she was unloved. (In fact she had no money problems worth mentioning, in reality, of which I was well aware.) The reality of her financial situation was, of course, the outer one; but in her inner world she felt like a hungry orphan, poor. Here was an important contradiction, which I encountered frequently.

Just before our time was up, this young woman started bargaining. I pondered whether I had, after all, produced some tiny inner shift in her rigid attitude. 'Very well', she began condescendingly, if I insisted she would see a psychotherapist, even if she had to pay, but she would only have a session once a week and that was that. I replied that this would be a self-defeating exercise. So great was the hostility with which she was now flooding me in a 'bad mother' transference that I felt certain that once a week would merely be colluding with her deeper secret purposes to keep a therapist as 'bad' and, above all else, impotent; this would justify her grievances and keep her envious feelings at bay. These would have to surface, I knew, if the therapist could be experienced as a helpful figure, and surface in due course they would, however painful the experience. Nonetheless it was essential in order to effect some change in the deeper layers of her mind in the course of therapeutic work. Her approach was clearly neither fair to a therapist or to herself. At best, a stalemate would ensue; at worst, I feared, catastrophe. These details of my reasoning I could not, at this stage fully share with her. Here we both depended on a modicum of mutual trust which, as I had half expected, was not forthcoming from her side. She declined to agree to sessions three times a week with ill-concealed outrage. I sensed how she had manoeuvred me into becoming a 'controlling and greedy mother with an expertise born of lifelong practice'. Subsequently, it turned out that since she was privately insured, the overdose had landed her in a private hospital where there was no need to pay! That would teach me to suggest that she should be paying fees!

Do I feel in retrospect responsible for these events which might have ended with her death? These in-depth assessments can resemble explorative surgery and we are certainly involved in a major intervention if this important dialogue is to produce some food for thought, in other words to bear fruit. I felt, on subsequent reflection, that this intelligent young woman had set up this interview to provide the final proof that no-one really cared for her; she might as well, she felt, be dead. In my steadfast attitude she saw control and not concern. Her experience of our dialogue was of a battle of two wills between a mother and her daughter, where the mother had to win. I did not see this at the time, as far as I recollect. We learn as we go along. All experience is hard bought and we are always running behind schedule throughout the course of human life. It may be regrettable, but it is nonetheless a fact which we have to come to terms with, whatever our vocation.

We have so far emphasized the simple act of listening to the actual spoken word although some reference has been made to an experience in the realm of our subjective feelings: for example, being 'flooded with hostility'. Listening to verbal content when we take a history may not get us very far along the road of deeper truth unless that receptivity from the realm of our feelings is harnessed to our intellect to constitute a faculty which we might call our inner ear, an instrument which we discerned in our personal therapy, an instrument no-one can see as they can see a stethoscope, but which is indispensable. Its nature is to resonate at the level of our intuition so that this may harmonize with the afore-mentioned functions to obtain our three-dimensional bearings. A mind which is not too disturbed is one that has become three-dimensional at the receiving end of maternal reverie. Given a good enough container, the infant mind will apprehend the nature of inner space. It will, as we might say, unfold, through one and two dimensional stages. This delicate and subtle process can also move into reverse. Under intolerable pressures the mind collapses and folds up, like a tent in a gale. Here is the condition which mystics frequently describe as 'the dark night of the soul' when, as

St Theresa said, she had to wait patiently to hear again 'the voice of God'.

A psychotherapist will know that when his mind-tent blows down, however fleetingly, during an assessment, it has come under attack by the mind of a patient who is seriously disturbed. We hope that it will not blow down altogether. The canvas may begin to flap, the ropes come under bouts of pressure, but hopefully the whole will hold, where the therapist's own mind has been fortified and stabilized during his training therapy. Then these squalls, which are caused by the patient's projections during the interview, can be read as can the weather by a meteorologist who, we hope, will be able to stand firm on both his feet and not be routed by a gale.

With the girl I described above, I came under more serious attack than I made full allowance for. Where a patient may be very intelligent or have other talents of some note, or where we may become seduced into a sudden, powerful liking for a certain individual, we may deny our experience of being crucially disturbed during the interview; we may be unable to face all the implications that this disturbance must have for the ultimate prognosis. This was, I think, another factor, which must have sidetracked me in my hour with this patient. I was filled with admiration for her accomplishments within her chosen field, in the face of her inner difficulties, and at a time when she was so young. Certainly in this respect her predicament resembled an earlier one of my own. Such matters, if we are not careful, can catch us out at any time, especially if we are fatigued.

What precisely happens where we get 'flooded' or 'swamped' or seriously disturbed as we take a history? Where we cannot relate our own threatened state of mind simply with the verbal content, even where it may convey momentous personal tragedy? Almost certainly, a patient who affects us in this way is seriously out of touch with his own inner feelings. For where we have individuals who can talk about the conflicts which they feel inside themselves, who can describe experiences which disturb and trouble them, our task is not too difficult; we remain in possession of our faculties and, above all, we are able to think with sufficient clarity. Yet our deeply troubled patient may have a two-dimensional mind which cannot contain the feelings that give rise to conflict or perhaps to psychic pain. The patient has, in fact, acquired the habit of splitting off unwanted feelings and then getting rid of them by projection into others (the history-taker in this case). Before the history-taker knows just what is happening, he will suddenly begin to feel rather peculiar: stupid, no good, helpless or murderous, perhaps half-asleep or as if floating (to mention just a few examples). If the note-taker admits it, which may or may not be the case, he will also feel quite scared, rather as though bewitched. What has happened? Why this feeling of being depersonalized, no longer knowing who he is, and threatened in some uncanny way? The nightmare situation feels alarmingly familiar. What our young psychiatrist, or his senior colleagues, for that matter, probably do not know about, are the infant terrors which the sufferer is pushing out in a wild and forceful stream in order to get rid of them, with the inner conviction that his survival is at stake.

These are feelings which belong to our earliest infancy, where they were legitimate. Where maternal provision falls below a minimum, the infant will not survive. Where the failure applies mainly to the container function, or maternal reverie and not to physical care, survival may be conditional upon degrees of mind-arrest. Each of us can, in our heart, once we get in touch with it, locate this universal fear that death will overtake us with our basic life-task undermined by defaulting faculties before these have been remedied. But unless we have explored these terrors in self-scrutiny of personal psychotherapy, their projection into us will probably initiate anxiety so severe that our mind takes to flight when it should be at its post. It may not even stop at that, for such a history-taker may even become quite vindictive, so that the interview ends in hopeless, self-defeating ways. The sufferers may not return. They may feel that they have harmed the psychiatrist, just as in infancy they felt, in their omnipotence, that they must have harmed their mother if she failed them in respect of maternal reverie. Or patients may ask for ECT as a form of punishment for having caused such awful feelings in the poor psychiatrist. In other words the outcome may take sado-masochistic forms, by an act of collusion. In the case of the patient from whose notes we have quoted the decision to refer him to a psychotherapist was not a creative one born out of true dialogue as a joint choice and decision, but an act of exorcism by a psychiatrist who was surely scared out of his wits.

Let us now look at some extracts from the therapist's reply to the referring colleague:

This young man with long, unbrushed hair, sallow face and hopeless eyes looked deeply and chronically depressed. What is more this depression virtually oozed out of him, threatening to drown us both. He reiterated aggressively that he had been seeing double since X had, out of the blue, left him six weeks ago after eight years of living together 'as close as could be'. All he now wanted out of life was to take care of their son, Y, aged six. But his eyes, of course, prevented that. This had left him with no choice other than to go back home to Mum.

I broke into this make-believe by interrupting him to say that I found this rather strange, that he was seeing pretty well for ordinary purposes and that the eye specialist had found no reason for concern. 'I'm not going to leave my son', he repeated drearily. I was filled with angry disbelief in this version of the story and said I did not have the feeling that what he was telling me carried conviction for himself; had he perhaps not felt depressed for quite a part of his life? He lapsed into angry silence and cowered behind a wall of possibly lifelong grievances.

His childhood story, colourless, toneless, vague, rings
hollow and is not to be trusted in terms of emotional
actualities. The despair which he projected almost certainly
belongs to very early deprivation. He is the third of four
sibs, all at three year intervals. He recalls seeing his
youngest brother, through the bars of a hospital cot, since
his brother was hospitalized with pneumonia shortly after
birth. He said he had no recollection with regard to how
he felt concerning that experience, which could well
explain one root cause for early depression in terms of
deeper anxieties that he had caused the baby's illness
with his hostile phantasies.

School held neither terror nor joy. He made friends, he
claims. The kind of 'friends' he would later describe
himself as drinking (heavily) with through desolate, dark
evenings. I felt that he did not know what the word
'friend' meant.

After leaving home at 17 following one of the habitual
rows with father, he camped in dingy bedsits with a
record player and evenings of drinking, parties and girls.
He worked as a plumber's mate, then in the rag trade, on
his own account, and later in antique restoration, where
he is still completing a first apprenticeship. This, his
present work, he likes. It sounds faintly like a first
potentially genuine reparative task and may be the only
factor staving off a total regression at this stage, back to
merging with a 'close as can be' early symbiotic mum,
whom he never really left.

This feeling is confirmed by his description of life with
X, as just 'magic', and 'close as can be, never apart day
or night' until the baby which she wanted 'put her off him
and sex', perhaps like the baby brother came between
himself and Mum, until he was hospitalized.

He is full of grievances over X's desertion for which he
seems to see no cause. 'I gave her everything. All those
years of my life.' He is totally baffled by her moving out,

totally out of touch with his or her real feelings all these years. That she might have been unhappy he denied emphatically, with his bland hostility. When I asked him whether he could be a little more precise as to what exactly he felt that he gave her he repeated, 'all those years and records'. Filled to the brim with his feelings of utter impotence and total inner emptiness I suggested that he felt empty and pretty hopeless about himself, that perhaps he felt as though he had nothing good to give, as matters stood, and without help. He agreed briefly and then said, 'no'. It was not true. Why was I putting ideas into his head? He was loving and caring until the day she left. Loved the child. Took him to the park. Yes, sometimes, in the afternoon. Yet on closer scrutiny their life together came across as colourless, joyless: deadly.

I suggested that if the 'magic' got lost he had perhaps felt pushed out by the baby. He denied this too and repeated that he loved the baby, that he did his share of the chores and was loving and caring as could be. As if to prove it he added, 'I now pay Mum for my keep; I pay her a fiver a week.' 'What else do you do for Mum?' I asked. There was no answer to that. After his evening meal he leaves for the pub until closing time. I suggested a little lamely that we had now spent over an hour together and that perhaps he had left all the chores to me and not done much of his share here. He agreed, to my surprise, and added that he had, in fact, been more forthcoming than usual. I felt that he was demanding signs of my appreciation for giving me so many words. Since this was not forthcoming, he lapsed into total silence now. I sensed he felt that I would shortly walk out on him, just like X, for no reason other than the way that mothers will walk out and see to another baby. This man is certainly not ready to think of joining a group. The reality of an 'other' is no concept for him yet. I said that we might meet again to try and explore things further if he should decide to make a further appointment at his own, expressed wish.

This report does not provide a detailed assessment from a psychodynamic point of view. But at least we get a feeling of a human situation and profound predicament. We can appreciate that here is a case of mind arrest and a life situation which is seriously stuck, predictably, in consequence. We can see quite clearly that this unhappy man is far from ready to take responsibility for the psychotherapeutic task, even to take the smallest share that we could expect in the beginning. At this moment of his life, he still chooses to play a game. The game is called 'seeing double'. Yet he is far from ready to 'see' that there are two of him: the self-idealized façade in which he has encased himself and an angry, helpless infant who wants to be taken in and sheltered from a hostile world. That this world, in fact, is filled with his own hostile feelings born of countless frustrations which he projects into it, is something we would not expect him to acknowledge at this stage.

Yet even in this hopeless man, drugged to the eyeballs as he was, I would not be surprised to hear that certain comments which were put forward by the psychotherapist may have fallen onto better soil than was apparent at the time. For there is no such thing as a truly hopeless case, even where the present looks rather less than promising. Even here, we found a plus. He liked his present work: the restoration of antiques. In all the darkness which prevailed, we found this creative spark smouldering on undeterred. For all we know it is waiting to become a little flame. But our limited resources must be put at the disposal of those sufferers who show a greater readiness for the therapeutic task.

We have here come up against an obvious, crucial limitation in our particular approach. Psychotherapy demands that at the very least one part of the personality, which we speak of as the 'adult' part, is strong enough to make a contract with the psychotherapist, based on aims and

objectives, on a genuine wish to grow, and on the acknowledgement that such growth requires change which in turn
may be painful, as growing pains are. Such a wish may be
based on considerable suffering acknowledged in the status
quo of a self-defeating lifestyle. It will often take time,
perhaps years of recurring crisis or of humiliating setbacks,
to really crystallize out from a general morass of inner
darkness and despair, to find the way to the light from a maze
of subversive strategies which are known as defences and
reaction formations.

Before this chapter is concluded, I would like to illustrate
the anti-productive stalemate in psychiatry today with two
further examples which impressed themselves on my mind
and refused to go away. The first concerns a young mother
newly arrived from overseas where she had been a social
worker, who wanted psychotherapy and came to see me for
that purpose. I could see straight away, as she stood on the
doorstep, that hers was a wild and despairing state of mind.
It presently transpired that the youngest of her four children,
all of them under five, was now approaching four months old.
Somehow, she explained to me from behind long, tangled
hair, and weeping profusely all the time, she had not been
able to love this baby from the start: not as she had loved the
others. She simply had no inkling why. Now she kept
shaking, and she felt that she was going to collapse, or
worse, that she was heading for some absolute catastrophe.
Yes, it would happen any day; if she could only just stop
shaking and losing such a lot of weight. There we were on
an autumn morning. It was sunny, I recall. She filled me with
a dreadful fear and an increasing sense of panic. I felt that
something must be done and done this second or all was lost.
Yes, now I knew, that was it, that if we lost precious time
her little ones would lose their mother. No, she was not going
to die, but they would lose her all the same. These thoughts
went racing through my mind. There seemed no doubt she
was presenting me with a grave emergency, to which the

doctor in me responded; I had the temptation to step in as
the magical physician which was not easy to resist.

Only a few days ago, she continued her story, she had seen
a psychiatrist. He had sent her straight away, as a matter of
grave urgency, to see a hormone specialist who diagnosed
excess thyroid and prescribed a potent drug to try and set
the balance right. But since this drug 'went to the milk' the
baby must, he said, be weaned, at once, from one day to the
next. This had multiplied her dreadful guilt. This baby she
had never loved, the way she would have wanted to, was now,
it seemed, to be deprived of her mother's breast as well. But
they had given her no choice. It was not her habit to question
high authority and she had done as she was told. The drug
was also dangerous. It might, the specialist had warned her,
even cause leukaemia. Constant check-ups were required.
The thought of blood tests every month only multiplied
her terror. By the time she came to me she had been on this
drug for just a week.

I sat and listened carefully. I was a psychotherapist and
not a doctor any longer in that comfortable old sense, with
back-up from laboratories, X-ray departments and so forth.
Whatever aspects of this dire emergency concerned me
here, I had to find them in the mind, though to locate them
in the body, as my two colleagues had done, was very
tempting, certainly. All things considered, I could see why
that psychiatrist had resorted to prompt action and tried to
get her off his hands, for her terror simply swamped the room,
threatening to wash us both away. It was not easy to sit tight.
And yet I knew that my job was to try and understand the
deeper meaning of her story in the depths of my own mind.
She had come to me for help because some part of her
suspected that such a meaning must exist, if we could only
reach it, by putting our two minds together.

Then slowly it began to dawn in my mental hinterland,
as I let her rampant panic penetrate it gradually, that the
nature of her fear was, in fact, of going mad. Having slipped

into this truth, my own anxiety was lessening so that I had more mental space in which to build up her story as the details of her life unfolded for my benefit. She herself, I heard her saying (my deeper listening restored rather more effectively), had also been her mother's fourth. And, when she was four months old, her mother suddenly broken down with a serious mental illness, not in evidence before as far as anyone could tell. She had to be hospitalized for some months. What was more, this episode proved to be the first of many; her mother had begun a long career as mental patient, having, it seemed, been well up until then.

More clearly in the picture now, both the inner and the outer one, I could draw this woman's attention to her possible anxieties that history might repeat itself, that she would go mad after her fourth child as well. Her face cleared as by miracle. She shook her hair back, visibly relieved. A fine, intelligent young face revealed itself quite suddenly. 'How funny that they did not tumble to that in the hospital!' she said. I hardly thought it funny, but did not say so, at the time. Once our therapeutic work began to get underway, we very soon came up against her ever-deepening terror that she was going to drive me mad. But that is another story.

My final illustration comes from the story of a friend, an art restorer all his life. When he was in his early fifties his wife died under circumstances which were tragic almost beyond belief. Neglectful of all basic needs, unwashed, half-starved, numb with despair, self reproach and self hatred, he was eventually admitted to the local mental hospital. There, he was promptly put onto an array of drugs in quite distressing quantities. The psychiatrist would not explain what these were or how they worked. Perhaps he did not even know who his extinguished patient was. The pills, he claimed, would make him well. They would put him on his feet again. At first he felt too ill to care. All that he wanted was to die. He also wanted to get well so he could get back to his child and live enough to carry on and heal his sorrows with his work. He told me, some years afterwards, how four or five times every day, this great big trolley came around full of potions, capsules and pills, which two nurses then dished out to a long, obedient queue. The procedure loomed like a ritual of archaic healing rites, like worship of a deity, as he saw it initially in his dim and woolly state. And the woolliness increased. Soon, he began to have difficulties with his sight. The fat was truly in the fire. In a great state of alarm and total panic, he complained to this same psychiatrist, who told him, 'Yes, it happens with these drugs. It is among their side-effects.'

'In that case I have to stop them because my eyesight is my life. Without it I'm completely lost. I might as well go hang myself.'

'It is hardly our intention, sir, to make our patients blind.' The psychiatrist was clearly very hurt and displeased by this show of insurrection. 'You are of course very depressed,' he reminded the patient grandly, blow for blow.

'I would rather be depressed,' said the patient, 'than be blind.'

'In that case, you'll need ECT.'

This he did not wish to have. Other patients had complained of their failing memory after the treatment. Therefore, he refused to sign his permission and consent. Presently a nurse appeared and said he needed an injection whose nature she did not explain. He thought in retrospect that it was very likely valium. 'I was as high as a kite,' he told me very angrily. 'I would have signed my life away.' Years later, telling me this tale, back in his studio, he still felt bitter that he had suffered this assault or rape before he took his own discharge. Today, this man is still depressed. 'The circumstances of my life are hardly cheerful,' he admits. Still, he is standing on the bridge of his shattered life again. During the hours he devotes to his art restoration, his suffering is held at bay. His only child is doing well. Life, however sorrowful, holds some meaning once again.

My friend had managed to retrieve a sense of his autonomy. He had chosen to decline the fetters of custodial care by telling his custodians that even if his life had stalled it was still *his* life, not theirs, that if his need was for asylum for a certain interlude, this need was for a breathing space, until his own battered engines could find a spark to start up again. That he *would* start up again he had never entirely doubted.

Freud himself was precisely up against a tradition of custodial care which he began to cut across by giving birth to new ideas; it is in the light of his ideas that a sufferer can retain autonomous dignity, under their protection that he can exercise free choice and turn to a method of support which thankfully has freed itself of punitive vindictiveness, however carefully disguised, and archaic hocus pocus. Freud, of course, did not conjure his new laws of the unconscious simply out of thin air, although we like to think that genius waves that famous magic wand. Ideas invariably possess an intricate pre-history, provided we can trace it back. God may say, 'let there be light', but man delves slowly in the dark tunnelling towards new day, because we must *become* the light, so that we can *live* our truth. For this we know we will be hounded, a price we are prepared to pay, since every thinker knows the ground of the void of loneliness. This desert has become his home. Accustomed to those wide horizons, the habitat of the mystic, he is finally beyond the temptation to recant, as the New Testament confirms. For did Jesus not retreat into the same wilderness from which not even Satan could lure him with a bribe of gold.

The leap Freud took was to approach the obscure phenomena of the mind not only in his troubled patients but steadfastly in his own self. By such means, he relegated the psychiatry of his time, and as we know it still today, permanently to the past. He gave the human mind its future, and we may not turn back the clock.

2

Towards a Method

Freud walked onto the stage of the drama of the human mind when the idea of cause and effect, newly rooted in the sphere of general medicine by that time, as we shall shortly see, stood ready waiting in the wings to make an impact on psychiatry. To reach this moment had required unerring courage and great personal risks from earlier workers in the field. Conservatism rules supreme in the kingdom of ideas, and it was safer to kowtow to previous assumptions that the soul is an elixir which must be redeemed by acts of God than to suggest that the mind obeys the rule of certain inner laws, even if these were still obscure. Substitute God for psychochemistry, and there is little change today in the ivory towers of psychiatry.

In earlier days, lunatics were deemed possessed by the devil for their sins. The Church proclaimed its determination to stand firm to the last drop of its blood; its men of faith were not to know how close to their ideology metapsychology would be in less than a single century, that it would clearly demonstrate how the drama of man's inner world is the lifelong battle waged between our human love and hate, between our love and our despair, sanity and lunacy – inner death or inner life.

So let us take a brief look back. Let us have an inkling of where we have come from in so short a time. In 1603, Edward Jordan published a book: A *Brief Dicourse of a*

Disease Called The Suffocation Of The Mother. Mother was the term for womb, as well as female parent. Jordan set about the writing of this work as an act of sympathy with one Elizabeth Jackson who had stood trial in the previous year before the Lord Chief Justice Anderson at London sessions for having bewitched a girl of 14, Mary Glover, whereby the latter had fallen into 'fittes . . . so fearful, that all that were about her supposed that she would dye'. At various times, the girl was rendered 'speechless, and blynde . . . her necke and throat did swell . . . depriving her of speeche . . . the left hand, arms and whole side were deprived of feeling and moving . . . her belly, shewed . . . certain movings' (Fleury, 1900). Jordan was clearly not impressed by the witch-hunt ambience that these emotive texts convey. An enlightened scepticism underlay his own approach. But he was also a careful man who did not want his own head on a block, and therefore he prevaricates before the Church and its impending wrath with an opening sop. He writes that he would not deny that the ways of God towards his children 'worke extraordinarily', but that he would 'in the feare of God' nonetheless still suggest that the cause may not be possession but the 'effects of natural disease so strange to such as have not looked thoroughly into them'. Almost four centuries ago and long before this could be proved, he postulated, at great personal risk, rational explanations here, even if he had no hope of demonstrating them as yet. Others would reach that promised land. He was prepared to prophesy and to support a lonely girl.

Jordan, as we can see today, was heroically grappling with the phenomenon of hysteria. He was prepared to look behind the full furore of appearances; it still takes a brave person in our day to defend the ground of findings against the clamour of a world bent on 'evidence' and 'quick results': as certain scientists today. Is it not therefore just as well that those who set out to explore the secrets of our inner world were not sidetracked or seduced by unruffled surfaces? For even if we

like to think that we are living in 'enlightened' days, we only
have to take one step beyond the warehouse of ideas-in-stock
to have that fond illusion smashed over our simplistic heads.

Let us leave Jordan now and skip 250 years ahead, to the
mid-nineteenth century. Around that time, when Freud
was born, we find ourselves in an epoch of wonders in
medicine generally. Semmelweiss, that great Hungarian
obstetrician, by getting his students to wash their hands in
a solution of chlorinated lime before examining women in
childbirth had reduced the deaths from childbed fever from
18 percent to 3 percent at the time. For this he was derided
and attacked by other physicians in his native Budapest
and died in an insane asylum of the very infection in the
blood, known as septicaemia, to whose prevention he himself
had dedicated his own life. That this prevalent and recurring
form of death had a clear, demonstrable cause which people
could themselves remedy, amounted still to heresy.

But if there were casualties in the running fight for truth,
reinforcements were being brought up from all sides to be
thrown into the battle against the forces of superstition and
wilful ignorance. Louis Pasteur had shattered the cherished
belief that alcohol was formed by some unknown, mysterious
and semi-religious influence. He was able to show that
fermentation arose from a fungus which grew on the outer
surfaces of grapes and gave them their bloom (Lapage,
1964). The connection between many diseases and microor-
ganisms or bacteria was being established step by step. As
Edward Jordan had prophesied, acts of God were fading out
dramatically on every side and being replaced by rational
explanations. Koch was growing the bacilli of anthrax in pure
culture now and laying down the basic laws of bacteriology.
Even consumption, later known as tuberculosis, was found
to have a bacillus as its cause. Meanwhile, Pasteur was
tackling rabies, and produced a vaccine against this as well.
And so by the 1880s, medicine was presided over by the
microscope. Here it was proved beyond all doubt through

the medium of the eye, augmented by a new instrument, that neither magic nor mysterious retribution for men's sins, but living organisms caused these everyday illnesses of which such countless numbers died and which in epidemic forms could decimate whole areas. But what about psychiatry? What were the doctors doing here for those who had been deemed possessed?

Our year is 1885. We are in Paris at the gates of the famous Salpêtrière. In this gaunt infirmary, destined to stand as monument in psychiatric history, Charcot was devoting himself to the curiosities known as hysteria. 'He took the simplest facts, the easiest to observe; he rejected all the others, and in everything proceeded with extreme slowness and precaution, thus proving that he loved truth, contrariwise to those who prefer mystery, and that he possessed the precious gift of patience' (Fleury, 1900). Charcot was imperturbable:

'We shall leave aside,' he said, 'what are called the higher phenomena of magnetism, second sight, divination, the transmission of thought . . . When we find ourselves facing a phenomenon which captivates us by its strangeness, we will wait, if we do not feel that our knowledge is yet ripe enough for competent study of the case. There is nothing to hurry us; that which we shall not have been able to do, our successors will accomplish, for they will be armed with all that we shall have achieved.'

While the neurologists, in their frock-coated ranks, continued to believe in 'magnetic fluids' as the precipitating cause of wild disturbance in their gloomy wards, Charcot stood his ground. With infinite patience he surveyed simple, rudimentary facts from day to day and year to year, for as long as it might take for these obscure and tantalizing parts to fit themselves into a whole. Without reference to demonology or sorcery, painstakingly and humbly too, the master was extracting laws from a plethora of appearances. With this steadfast, sane approach, Charcot was forging the investigator's vigilance into an instrument, a tool with which to explore the actual phenomena at the expense of preconceived ideas. In this staunch manner, which relied on the five senses joined to common sense and nicely harnessed to the intellect, Charcot presided over the approach to the realm of the unconscious mind, the unknown but suspected hemisphere.

Can we be wrong if we assume that it was ultimately these exemplary qualities of mind, as much as what they brought to light, which presently impressed themselves on the youthful Dr Freud, who like countless others from across the European continent had come as a pilgrim to the Salpêtrière in that autumn of our chosen year. Rock-like perseverance in investigating a single subject matter had hardly been characteristic of the young doctor from Vienna until then. Anxious to make a great name for himself and thereby to secure a fortune so that he could marry his betrothed, he had until this time in his career cast about him in a restless way, from subject to subject and theme to theme in quest of quick, spectacular results and with them, hopefully, renown. In the spring of 1881, at the age of 25, he passed his final medical exams. Over the next four years of clinical and research work, he made a succession of false starts. In this unsettled frame of mind he managed to obtain a grant and leave of absence from the hospital in Vienna to study with Charcot for a while. And in an elated mood, he left for Paris, visiting his fiancée Martha Bernays on the way.

'The Salpêtrière', writes Ernest Jones in his biography of Freud, 'could well be called the mecca of neurologists. Charcot had stalked through the old wards of the infirmary for chronic cases, marking off and giving names to a number of diseases of the nervous system in a most Adam-like fashion.' If he did not know it then, in the fullest and deepest sense, Freud recognized the work of a master. For Freud, we may conjecture, was at a crossroads in his life, not only

in need of a worthy theme to anchor his unfolding intellect, but also of a model of sufficient calibre. Was it perhaps in recognition that he had at last found a way to satisfy this deep need that he translated some of Charcot's texts into German? Was this labour an act of homage?

Freud had travelled to Paris as a physiologist whose work was at the research bench but within a few weeks, he announced his decision to withdraw from this uninspiring work to the fascination of the wards. The bedside from this hour on would for Freud, as for Charcot, be the only true laboratory. Fortune stood smiling in the wings. Not only this, but Freud had already been fortunate; by a previous stroke of luck, already in his student years he had come upon a sphere of influence which too would bear important fruit once Charcot's methodology had taken root. Both influences were required, we can say with hindsight now, to fertilize Freud's restless mind.

Freud's senior by some 14 years, Dr Joseph Breuer was an eminent physician and a man of science working in their native Vienna. He and Freud had met at the Institute of Physiology and, sharing the same interest, had presently become close friends. It happened that while Freud was doubtless supposed to be burning the midnight oil working for his final exams, his older friend lost no opportunity to tell his willing listener the details of a stirring case he was treating at the time. The case of Anna O. obsessed Breuer totally, and we can take it that he talked to Freud of very little else for a while, certain that he would always find the response for which he craved: a burning interest that matched his own. We will hear more of Anna O. For our present purposes let us remember that we are in the early 1880s now, and that this girl had fallen ill while nursing her father. She suffered from twilight states, from paralyses and other incapacities which came and went in baffling ways. Dr Breuer, whom the family had consulted, had been treating her with a contemporary mixture of baths, suggestions and hypnosis for some weeks when an important innovation found admission into these stolid and relatively unproductive proceedings. Anna found that she gained most relief if her physician permitted her to talk at length of everything that troubled her. All that he himself had to do was sit and listen by the hour and sometimes to comment as best he could. The patient gave the name of 'chimney sweeping' to these long confessionals which rambled over many themes; she would await her doctor's visit and the anticipated relief, brief as it invariably proved, with impatience, day by day.

Breuer's fascination grew until one day he awoke to the recognition that his total preoccupation with the startling phenomena of this intriguing case was leading to jealousy and a morose withdrawal on the part of his wife. Conscience stricken, the physician informed his patient that he was going to terminate her treatment and fled in horror when she, at this prospect of being abandoned from one day to the next, developed an imaginary pregnancy and pursued him with wild declarations of love.

This was in 1882, and the story had made a profound impression on Freud at the time. But several more years were to pass before back from Paris, deeply imbued with the spirit of Charcot, and quite disenchanted with electropathy, baths, massage and hypnotism (the total package of the day), Freud eventually returned to Breuer's early method. Freud would let the patient talk. He would listen. Nothing more. Sit and listen by the hour . It was so simple that it seemed absurd: yet this came to be known as the Cathartic Method. The flow was at first encouraged by applying pressure to the patient's head, as if this helped the hidden memories to break out of their secret hiding place. The assumption at the time was still that buried memories of something noxious from the past must underlie these maladies.

How then, we will ask ourselves, sharing as we surely must, Freud's own impatience on the brink of his discoveries, was that transition to the true 'free association', whereby the

patient simply says whatever comes into his head, made? The
method was one which would become the very hallmark of
this new, unique procedure to be known as psychoanalysis.
A treatment which would also serve for research where
findings and theory go together hand in hand. It is free
association, which is bound to ensure that unconscious
content must use this uncensored flow to hitchhike to the light
of day.

There is a story that, in their long search for radium, the
Curies walked back together to the icy little shed which
served them as laboratory, to find their substance send a pale,
violet glow into the dark winter night. Neither had expected
such additional beauty as reward for their singlemindedness.
If such a moment came to brighten Freud's long, solitary
quest, it still lay 15 years ahead of him when he analysed
himself, and so stumbled inadvertently into the concealed
domain of infantile sexuality. But from the hour when he had
exchanged his place in the laboratory for the observation post
at the bedside, it would prove a step-by-step process of
discovery, through the span of a decade, to start to see the
light of day at hysteria's tunnel end. Between the 1880s and
the mid 1890s, the technique was steadily refined, as hypnosis
and suggestion, pressing the head and questioning were
gradually stripped away.

Watching his young colleague's painstaking but restless
thrust forward from the hocus pocus of an earlier, uncertain
age, Breuer wrote to their friend Fliess: 'Freud's intellect is
soaring at its highest. I gaze after him as a hen at a hawk.'
One of the fascinating aspects of the developing new
treatment, throughout its history, was the way patients would
contribute to take the method further on. Just as previously
Anna O. had initiated the idea of 'chimney sweeping' when
she talked, so, in 1892, Miss Elizabeth (whom we shall meet
later) remonstrated each time Freud would interrupt her flow
of words with a question, as he often did. With his extraordinary intuition and a scientist's humility Freud was glad to

take the hint. In this manner, by 1896, the term 'psycho-analysis' was employed for the first time in a paper by Freud. Of all the relics of the past, only free association and the famous couch remained, and are still, of course, used today.

Freud now had the first hints of a method with which the conscious human mind could approach that other part, the unconscious mind; an undiscovered hemisphere had opened up, at last, in front of a startled intellect. From this first foothold, it was to be what Meltzer subsequently called 'the spiral of method and data' which was very gradually to lead from those early faltering steps to strides along the highroad of a majestic discipline, landmark by landmark, mile by mile and by generations too. Today, the great great grand-children are working in those harvest fields and still maintaining that little more than the surface has been scratched. What, when all is said and done, is a single century? Is it a minute or an hour on the dial of the sun? How had this Freudian approach surpassed the old psychiatry of tidy labels and neat categories which are still to be found in the text books of today. By the illumination that symptoms have a deeper meaning. This was Freud's Rosetta stone. But like those sets of Russian dolls there are meanings within meanings until they touch infinity. For our present purposes we are going to ask ourselves what is the meaning of hysteria – the syndrome where it all began. For if symptoms have a meaning then so has the illness as a whole, whatever name it may go by. What, in essence, does it tell us about the individual patient and every other patient too? And once we have discovered that, what conclusions can we draw about its general, wider meaning for human beings of our time, since it is very likely that the sufferers whom we call patients pinpoint a general malaise.

In focusing on hysteria, we share in the excitement of the founder of a new era for the human race. Is not our first experience of the majestic work of Freud, that of the poet upon 'first looking into Chapman's Homer'? Even if that is far removed from what we shall be doing here, we may just catch the faintest flavour in what follows. There we will take a cursory look at the fledgeling in its nest which would later grow a mighty wing span: psychoanalysis.

Five Ladies with Hysteria

Hysteria is dying out.

This statement must be qualified. The fullblown drama of the past suited to Grand Opera is certainly on the decline. At least in those parts of the world where ladies have become women who walk around the streets in jeans.

Now we seldom come across a member of the female sex who draws attention to herself in startling and dramatic ways, then falls into some kind of trance only to come round again with one or more limbs paralysed or other disabilities creating general alarm. Such is the picture which the word hysteria tends to conjure up, although the illness will begin with more decorum, frequently, and has acquired rather more elaborate implications now.

When this phenomenon was prevalent it often occurred in the boudoir or the plush salon. Here the ladies of a certain class, kept in a gilded cage like birds, were afflicted as a rule. Their illness substituted for a genuine, creative life beyond a procreative one. But gilded cages still exist. Both in western families and farther regions of our earth individual lives are crippled by prevailing tyrannies; here among us they may be found as a sickly norm in maladjusted families which create an environment where mental illness may have thrived for several generations in sticky, sad obscurity.

When I was still a family doctor, friends asked me whether I would see a young lady from Ecuador. They said she was both beautiful and rich; she had, they told me, recently been swept off her feet by a famous singer from Madrid. He had then jilted her. As soon as she received the news, it seems

that she fell down paralysed, from the waist down to her feet.
When she had been carried back to her apartment she had
asked that the curtains should be drawn day and night, for
evermore. She had put a black turban on and only permitted
one dim light in the bedroom where she lay. I found her, at
this well-staged wake, with, of course, a private nurse who
was dressed by contrast all in white. The theatrical effect had
all the flair and the panache of a great designer's hand. Her
legs were clenched together tightly and were held entirely
straight, as in a single plastercast. Her heart was broken, she
explained, and would never mend again. She would remain
stricken down from now until her dying day. She said this
with a weary smile which never seemed to leave her face, with
its thick foundation cream. Fragrance of an expensive scent
hung around her small, slight form. No, she did not want to
have any medical attention. But would I, since I seemed so
kind, visit her from day to day, not as a doctor but as a friend?

I was not the only one; the situation which her friends
referred to as 'The Tragedy', was arousing copious interest
and neverending sympathy, with attention from all sides. No-
one in her circle worked. Ladies in expensive furs, shod
with airy-fairy shoes, took it in turn to visit her with roses,
chrysanthemums and white lilies wrapped in cellophane, or
with mysterious little gifts, sweetmeats and costly bric-à-brac
from London's most expensive stores. But as the days and
weeks went by these little shifts lost interest. Nothing had
been left unsaid about the villain of the piece. And very
probably there were new and more exciting things going on,
but somewhere else. More and still more frequently I found
the patient all alone, her sole companion the nurse.

At this low hour a man friend from an embassy, unable
to endure her plight, offered to take her home to his own
bachelor ménage. Again a whole new circle formed. Again
the full attentions boomed until he also wearied of the
responsibility of this business he had taken on. By now it
happened that we entertained certain suspicions as to what

might be the true state of affairs. A little powder dusted on
the kitchen floor soon provided evidence that when no-one
was around, she lifted herself up from her bed and walked.
After a few tactful hints, she ordered crutches for herself.
These charming new accessories she used with all the pretty
guile of a seductive little girl. And before a week had passed
these orthopaedic implements were left behind in Heathrow's
First Class Waiting Lounge.

The play would almost certainly be enacted somewhere
else with horrible monotony.

The childhood of this patient had been a classic of its kind.
Shuttled from one nanny and boarding school to another by
wealthy and inept parents, she had grown up with all the
equipment for a rewarding life but without a sense of
personhood, of being wanted for herself. Circumstances of
this kind, all too common as they are, may wipe the most
promising options out in cruel and self-defeating ways. To
lend some meaning to an empty life, such women lurch
from role to role; there always has to be a role or there is
nothing but a void. Confronting the void cannot be risked.
To risk it is to show a need for help, a need for others on the
terms of genuine relationship. This, as we have seen, must
rest on the confession to ourself, and to the other, that we have
needs and demands to satisfy if we are ever going to grow into
that which is our self, the goal and challenge of each human
life. For the alternatives remain as illness or as an empty role.

There may be successive roles which can include quite
dazzling ones, even significant success, but this will all feel
meaningless in that waxwork gallery where, in the earliest
months and years, the parent figures have retained the place
of subject to the child as object – as the merest thing –
however this has come about. Where it occurs, it confiscates
the options and possibilities which constitute a separate
life. True autonomy implies genuine subjectivity.

In the bourgeois Vienna of Freud's time, archaic despotism
ruled in family life as a norm, just as we find it still at work

in today's case histories, regardless of geography or class, flourishing side by side with the highlights of atomic science. The stories of the five ladies, which serve to illustrate this theme, are the subject of a book: *Studies on Hysteria*. Drafted in 1892, the book was duly published in May 1895, jointly authored by Breuer and Freud. The actual treatments all took place between 1880 and 1892, starting with Breuer's Anna O., whom we have already met. All of the women had this in common, that each was making some sort of bid, even if a misguided one, to achieve subject status in a confined and thwarted life. Each of them was endowed with a lively, active mind which she longed to call her own.

Breuer wrote of Anna O. that she in fact was 'bubbling over with intellectual vitality' when she fell ill. Her days had been devoted to nursing her father at the time. In the summer of 1880, her father had been taken ill with an abscess on the lung, of which he died the following spring. In the months before his death, the health of his devoted nurse started to deteriorate. She grew anaemic, pale and weak, began to lose her appetite and, around Christmas party time, developed a distressing cough. Deeply concerned, the family now called Dr Breuer in. But matters went from bad to worse. For while the doctor treated her, with the best prevailing tricks of baths and massage and the rest, her illness rapidly assumed a malevolent and crippling form. States of excitement came and went. She suffered headaches and a squint. Sometimes she could not move her head and, to make matters worse her right arm and leg were paralysed, suddenly, for several months. Only with her father's death the symptoms gradually improved, although just after he died everyone had cause to fear that the girl would kill herself. When the paralysis of her arm and leg set in, Anna had been keeping watch at her father's bed one night. She fell into a 'waking dream'. In this state she thought she saw a black snake coming from the wall towards the patient in her care, to bite the dozing, feverish man.

From my childhood in those parts I remember those black snakes with a vivid, golden cross. These *Kreuzotters*, as they were called, were held in superstitious dread; their bite, it was said, would lead to a quick and ugly death. To dream of one was nothing less than a death wish, we could say. But Anna's arm had gone to sleep, and in her trance-like state or dream she had felt unable to ward the deadly creature off. This was the episode which had brought the paralysis about which crippled her for several months.

Now, to the alarming cough. Keeping vigil once again in the quiet of the night, suddenly Anna heard music from a nearby house. Others were enjoying life. And it crossed her lively mind that she would rather go and dance than spend her evenings as a nurse. At this point she gave a cough and after that coughed every time that she heard music anywhere. A single note would induce a fit of coughing straightaway. Anna gradually improved to become one of the first social workers of the time. Step by step, she mobilized her considerable gifts to find a third alternative to illness or an object's life. But the conflict took its toll. The freedom which the girl had won was no more than a partial one. Perhaps she felt that to enjoy professional and married life would mean that she had asked too much. This second longing was repressed, making hers a partial cure. It had only been expressed fleetingly when she pursued Dr Breuer frantically with her phantom pregnancy.

The second patient, Frau Emmy von N., Freud began to treat himself in May of 1889. She was 40 years old at the time. Her childhood, we are told, had been rather an unhappy one. Her mother was severe and strict. Today we might say that the mother could not tolerate self-expression in a child, that she would tend to meet it with expressions of hostility until the girl became subdued. But in those days, a rebellious offspring was expected to be put very firmly in her place. At the age of 23, Emmy had managed to escape into a happy marriage to an elderly industrialist. He enjoyed a high position which, by proxy, she now shared, to some degree at any rate, since he was fatherly and kind. They had two daughters. However, he died after the second daughter's birth, of a sudden stroke. His death now left her in full charge of a thriving business. It seemed the road ahead lay clear to an independent life with many varied interests. But her mother had conditioned her to be an object as a child. And so the path in fact was blocked and she could not avail herself of this opportunity for taking life into her own two hands. Instead, she now fell ill with nervous symptoms of all kinds and was admitted to a nursing home, where Freud started seeing her.

She had, as she explained to Freud, a terror of white mice and rats. When she was still a little girl her brothers and sisters would throw small dead animals at her, on occasion, she complained. Freud gave the endearing name of *zoopsia* to this, to lend it some scientific weight. Further, she was terrified of asylums, it transpired. Cruel treatments, she believed, were handed out to inmates there. They were restricted and restrained in terrible and cruel ways, even possibly tied up.

Freud's treatment met with some success. After seven weeks of daily hypnosis and suggestions and reassurances she made an excellent recovery which meant that she could go back home. Relapses tended to take place when members of her family suffered illness and she feared that she would end up as their nurse, as was expected of dutiful daughters at the time. Obviously, a conflict raged in her deeper mind between wishing to be immobilized, rendered lifeless, and tied down as punishment for wanting to enjoy herself and come to life, and having the possibility of being the subject of her life, which brought on deep anxieties. We would understand today that the small, dead animals in fantasy could represent the siblings she deprived of life if she grew and seized her own joyfully with open hands. Concrete thinking would imply life envisaged like a cake. If A has more then B has less, which we encounter every day in our therapeutic work.

In those very early days a deep conflict of this kind could not be thoroughly resolved. And so the treatment ended with a degree of compromise. Emmy ran her business very well with absolute efficiency, and kept a correspondence up in several foreign languages. But the price she had to pay for exercising and enjoying her obvious capacities was restriction to the life of a semi-invalid at recurring intervals. Such was her conditioning, such was the structure of her inner world, and inner objects, as we say today, that even with the help of Freud she was not able to break free. Her liberation was blocked not just by society, standing for the 'outer' world, but by an 'inner' mother who remained restricting and severe. Again this treatment ended in a degree of compromise between the ill and healthy parts of her personality: between the choice of death and life.

The third woman, Miss Lucy R., came to Freud in 1892 when she was 30 years of age. An Englishwoman, Lucy was living as a governess in a factory manager's home. Two children who were in her care had lost their mother recently. She complained that she would smell burnt pudding every now and then, ever since she had received a letter from her mother to ask when she was coming home; at other times a nasty smell of cigarette smoke troubled her. That was all, she said to Freud. It soon transpired that both smells related to encounters with her employer some time back. Each occasion had dashed her hopes that he planned to marry her. Of this she had been unaware until Freud questioned her, for she had kept these longings secret even from her inmost self. On the other hand, she knew that if these dreams could not come true she would be going home one day to live as nurse-companion to her ageing mother, a prospect she did not relish. Once she understood the conflict, the painful symptom disappeared. She stayed on as a governess, relinquishing her hopeless dreams, and managed to enjoy her work, since it was now an act of choice.

Katerina, the fourth woman, was not a patient in the strictest sense. While resting in a mountain hut after a summer morning's climb, Freud was unexpectedly addressed by a servant girl. She enquired, whether he was a doctor, for she suffered from attacks of terrifying breathlessness and fears that she would suffocate. In connection with these panic states, she invariably caught sight of a horribly angry face. In the interview which followed certain details came to light. She had an uncle who had made sexual advances to the girl. These she had properly repulsed over a period of some months. But one day she had caught him in the act of sexual intercourse with her cousin Franziska and divulged the matter to her aunt. To the uncle's rage (the angry face) a divorce had followed. The indignant aunt had left her husband together with the pregnant girl to run the original mountain inn and had moved to this more lonely hut where Freud had met her on that day. Freud was able to show her how when she caught the two in bed, breathing heavily, perhaps, the wish could have crossed her mind: I hope she suffocates and dies. For she had reason to regret her own display of virtue now; how unfavourably her fate, in this isolated place, with a sad, embittered aunt, compared with Franziska's happier days, in her phantasy at least.

The last of our five ladies was Miss Elizabeth von R. Freud began to treat her in the autumn of 1892. She was 24 years old, and had suffered for two years from distressing pains in both her legs which made it difficult for her to walk. As was the case with Anna O., her symptoms had also begun while the patient served as nurse to her father who had died. But they grew more serious a little later when she nursed her mother who was going blind. At that time her brother-in-law, her sister and their family had moved from the vicinity. Very soon her sister died in childbirth very tragically.

In the treatment, it transpired that just before her father died Elizabeth had been involved in an early love affair.

Filled with guilt and with remorse as her father became
worse, she had decided to withdraw from this new
relationship. Instead she now indulged in dreams about a
husband for herself such as her fortunate sister had. Secretly,
as it transpired, she nurtured a romantic love for her
forbidden brother-in-law until, upon her sister's death the
thought had flashed into her mind that now that he was freed
again, they might go walking as before. But no, her mother
needed her. Neither did the widower reciprocate her
cherished dreams. Nevertheless, the girl improved and later
married someone else. Freud tells us very charmingly how
he saw her at a ball go whirling past him happily.

Here, then, we have five vignettes from a previous century.
They come to us with the musty scent of the sick rooms of
the time, the scene of psychoanalysis in its first decade.
Where do these fragments leave us for our present purposes
today? Had these five patients fallen into rather more
conventional hands, they would have been, not Wards of
Court, but of psychiatrists, who would have disposed of
them in any one of various ways that were in fashion at the
time: hot baths; cold packs; exhortations; hypnotism – all the
tricks which preceded ECT and our plethora of pills. Instead,
they were privileged to become collaborators in the adult, new
approach of psychoanalysis, even if with hindsight it may
seem the work of amateurs. 'This was my first attempt at
handling that therapeutic method,' Freud was to write many
years later of his treatment of Mrs Emmy von N. 'I was still
far from having mastered it; in fact I did not carry the
analysis of symptoms far enough, nor pursue it systematically
enough.' Even so, these patients scrambled, in varying
degrees, out of the chronic invalidism which might otherwise
have been their fate. Some of them, as we have seen, went
forward in their personal growth. Others retrieved their way
of life instead of sliding down the slippery slope of involution
which can follow where evolution becomes blocked where
a patient is not helped to take responsibility for self-defeating

states of mind or where she slides or falls into those pater-
nalistic hands which will never help her find the means to
control her own destiny and life.

If the treatment and its results were both still in their
infancy we ought, nevertheless, to focus on that crucible
which is the actual relationship between the sufferer and the
therapist. Here, surely, lies one hallmark of the new
psychology compared to the old autocracy. Every single
patient knows, even if psychiatrists do not, that their
incapacity has a detailed history. If Freud's contemporaries
were 'inclined to regard the hysterical attack as a periodic
discharge of the motor and psychical centres of the cerebral
cortex', a jargon we still hear today, how was he to stand a
chance of getting his ideas across? 'I am tormented by the
problem of how it will be possible to give a two-dimensional
picture of anything that is so much of a solid as our theory
of hysteria,' he wrote to Breuer in 1892. How, at a time when
the study of neurology was relatively well advanced and
accessible to proof by the five senses which are given man
at birth, was he to persuade members of a conservative
profession that 'the memory which forms the content of a
hysterical attack is an *unconscious* one; or more correctly, it
is part of the second state of consciousness which is present,
organized to a greater or lesser degree, in every hysteria'? How
was he going to demonstrate that a new sense would have
to be developed as an instrument for psychological enquiry
in depth, and then to demonstrate it in action, in the same
way that the microscope could show bacteria which had
remained invisible to the naked eye?

In a letter to Breuer in the summer of '92, Freud had
referred to the 'unremitting pains of thinking'. As we
understand today, every new idea exposes each explorer to
pain if he wishes to assimilate this latest venue and expand
the mind. For just as muscles tend to ache with unaccustomed
exercise, so the mind protests as well as psychoanalysis has
found. It says: 'I'm tired', or 'I have all sorts of better things

to do', or 'Wasn't it all right before this latest nonsense came along?' It finds it easier to attack the source or person of this threat than go through all those labour pains. It would rather hold the baby back than be present at the birth which it did not initiate, out of envy, furthermore.

Freud harboured no illusions that these ideas which he was struggling for would be welcomed with open arms. And although his books were only burned later by the Nazis, they only put into effect covert opinions of the day, scarcely diminished in our own as the vociferous opposition continues to demonstrate. For the totalitarian mind is obstinately primitive and active within each of us, if to varying extent. We will look at this presently. Freud almost a century ago made his case that symptoms have a deeper meaning; yet psychiatry still continues to ignore this fact today, but goes on in its time-honoured fashion, awaiting a Messiah in the laboratory, one who will surely find the answer in a test tube and come up with the magic pill at last, since a firm belief in magic still lingers deeply in the psychiatric mind.

Freud felt, even in those earliest years, and during these initial treatments, that like Columbus he had now set foot on a new continent. But it was a mass without a map. His studies represent going ashore to establish bearings, inch by inch. Today we have more detailed maps, but we are painfully aware that generations still to come may think them very primitive. If Freud's studies marked the start of painstaking clinical research, our bird's-eye view can offer us something of a wider notion; in each case, the patient struggled, if in a misguided way, to achieve the status of becoming the subject of her life, a struggle which was waged against inner as much as outer forces. Now the actual struggle could hardly be responsible for the fracas which ensued, and must be laid at the door of symptom formation.

Freud was clear in his own mind that symptoms always represent an attempt at compromise in a deeply buried conflict. Mental illness, we could say, is an attempt at the impossible: to solve and also escape painful conflicts in our life. The battle in each case is between evolution or involution, between growth and sliding backwards, between what amounts to Life, and inertia – Death. We have to be quite clear on this crucial content of the drama all mental illness represents: there is no side-stepping this truth. A patient may arrive and moan, 'I am seeing double, doctor'. Or, 'Doctor, I begin to cough every time I hear music'. Or, 'I break out in a sweat when I travel in the tube'. But we have to be aware that in these familiar openings, there are two people addressing us who are locked into a bitter battle. One is saying, 'Doctor, please, make this terror go away with any means at your disposal provided that the cure is quick and puts me out of misery'. A second voice is pleading, although perhaps more quietly or drowned by the other's shouting, 'Doctor, help me to understand what is going on inside me when I want to hit my child, or feel hopeless and depressed though I have everything to live for. I do not mind how much it hurts or what price I have to pay to be master in my house and live as well as others can.' Which side of this conflict will the psychiatrist support?

In the health service at present, for every nine hours provided by orthodox psychiatry there is a single hour of psychotherapy offered in terms of equal expertise, in other words of consultant time. This ratio speaks for itself. But we get what we ask for. There is little doubt of that. On the other hand, in the London area, one Centre for Psychotherapy has around 500 patients coming for help each single year, many of them self-referred. This is only one instance; such centres multiply, sadly, however in the private sector. In the London area alone, hundreds of psychoanalysts and psychotherapists are busy, often working round the clock, but mainly in the private sector. Some of these work part-time in the National Health Service as well, to make up the ten per cent we were speaking of above. Many of them would be happy to increase their salaried hours, for a variety of reasons – their social conscience above all. Meanwhile, we find men and women drawn from many walks of life coming for this special help, to understand themselves and their deeper, buried conflicts.

At an initial interview, they come with many different stories. It may be that physical symptoms form the tip of the iceberg. These may be physical sensations for which medicine found no answer after long investigations: feelings that the heart will stop or that breathing is obstructed, dizziness or fears of falling. The person may complain that he or she has difficulty in making close relationships, in loving or in feeling deeply. People sometimes come along who say they feel they are not getting as much from life as they would like to. They sense that there are inhibitions which they feel unable to define, while longing for a remedy. Others may bring a very unhappy history; where we may feel that Job is speaking; there are tales of suffering which can almost break one's heart, lives which have been so self-defeating that one can only marvel at how sufficient hope was kept alive to bring a sufferer to this quiet door, after decades of tribulation: prison sentences perhaps, or years in mental hospitals. Here one can only bow one's head in wonder and humility that one is chosen as a guide for a project which is invested with such dread and hope and doubt.

It may seem that we have wandered a long way from hysteria. But Freud is never far away, seeing that he mapped the high road through this latest underworld, this modern version, if you like, of Orpheus and Eurydice. In our next chapter, we will look more closely at the theories which are based on the findings and the clinical experience gained through psychotherapy. For in this field, clinical findings have built the theory brick by brick. There is no idle speculation; only observation counts in this extraordinary work. The end in view is sanity. A word which can now be defined as that voice of the conflict which is on the side of life.

Those who enter psychotherapy wishing to exchange their suffering for a richer, 'happier life', have at that moment little inkling what they are really hoping for. If we told them at this stage that it is sanity which they are bidding for, many would feel quite offended. Most of us have no idea how far from sanity we live our daily unexamined life, how far from life affirmation, how close to Death with its inertia; and all the while we could be wide awake and alive.

3

The Cornerstones of Sanity

Human conflicts, great and small, centre around privilege. Whether it is children squabbling that this, that or the other 'is not fair', strife in politics or nations at each other's throats in war, this deeper dispute smokes and smoulders and keeps bursting into flame: who is going to be entitled to which goodies, when and where? Our reason may call them 'means of production', a home in the west or a sacred lake, but at the heart of the controversy lies the deeper dream of a wrong to be redressed. For human beings go through life with the sense that they have lost something which must be retrieved either in this life or the next; it resides in our phantasy as a kind of blissful, perfect state we were deprived of long ago by some villain, if only we could track him down.

This first and earliest privilege is, of course, the mother's breast. If offers nourishment and love with a generosity that nothing throughout later years is ever likely to surpass; when, in our infant helplessness, our very life depends on this. It also offers understanding, as we stress continuously, which is crucial if the mind is to grow into one piece sufficiently to hold together through the demands which lie ahead, the conflicts in our inner world as well as the exigencies the outer will keep throwing up. Food and love flow together provided everything goes well, when that link becomes embedded deeply in the matrix of our earliest experience.

Such a child becomes a person who is content and satisfied in the sense that he will not have an inner axe to grind dating from this earliest phase.

This is not to say that he is going to let marauders have the upper hand, or that in adult life he will not fight for social change; he will, though, be an individual who is not always out to wrest a brother's or sister's share and who tries to further equitable solutions. On the other hand, where food and love are split apart and earliest experience becomes fragmented in this way, the quest for material privilege often tends to run amok and become a tyranny without concern or true respect for another individual. During psychotherapy, this split and other fragmentations which have followed in its wake, can be slowly brought together. For this process, which evolves through a protracted span of years, offers a second infancy for all the changes time has rung – within a truly steadfast love. The love referred to is not Eros but his sibling, Agape, which means the gaping mouth, expectant and wondering.

Sanity stems from Sanus, health. Health has, from the start, first and foremost been understood as the prerogative of the mind. These matters have been known about since the dawn of the human race, since we came onto the stage of evolution's marathon. 'Known' in this sense would apply to our deeper preconceptions. These lie in readiness to mate with 'realizations', to become concepts in the conscious mind, as was clarified by Bion, a follower of Mrs Klein of whom we shall have more to say.

With this preamble, we return to the cornerstones of sanity. A cornerstone is normally something we can clearly see. On the other hand, we may have to dig it up to see it, and this requires an instrument. The mind can obviously not be seen with the naked eye, nor with the microscope, nor with the brain scan or whatever technology may devise. It can only be examined with a subtler instrument, nothing other than the mind itself, made sensitive for that purpose by the extended scrutiny known as psychotherapy. This is not the mind we are born with, nor the one which has been expanded by later learning, but, beyond that point, a mind which submitted itself freely as an object worthy of investigation and improvement.

This tradition of discipleship is, of course, an ancient one, rooted in dissatisfaction with what one is and what one undertakes, in terms of effectiveness as well as of surplus suffering. This is invariably the issue which brings each sufferer to seek for help in psychotherapy. The fellowship of suffering is, our basic human lot. It can never be escaped. But because of Freud's discoveries, and with the developments that have followed, we are in a position to transform its premises at last. This is the living fulcrum on which these labours rest today, that the suffering of the many different ailments of the mind in all their many degrees are unacceptable compared with the suffering we achieve once integration has progressed during psychotherapy.

This deserves further explanation. One kind of suffering could be described, in more simplistic terms, as being taken ill at night in some unfamiliar place, far from home and quite alone, with painful spasms in the dark, doubting that we will survive or be functional again. The second kind is that same scene transformed when the morning light has come. A doctor has arrived, a diagnosis has been made, treatment is underway and we find ourselves co-opted to a partnership in charge of something comprehensible, concerning which steps can be taken to lend fresh meaning to our life. We have gained new qualities of calm and growing inner strength which we did not possess before and a partner at our side; presently, this partner will find a place within our hearts, someone with whom to face whatever comes, knowing that we will not be spared the ordeal of psychic pain but that we will not be written off in frightening or malicious ways, as may have been the case in infantile experience.

Naive as this distinction seems, it contains certain elements which we need to understand regarding our development in the earliest months of life, when the cornerstones of sanity are gradually being laid, to ensure stability and mental equilibrium (if to varying degrees).

Let us take a closer look at these two predicaments. The first is dark, the second light. The first is solitary and strange, never-ending, full of fear of loss of crucial faculties and perhaps of life itself. In the second, there is help – an other – we are not alone. We have bearings. There is hope and understanding, above all, with the expectation that things will clarify still further. Gone is the sense of helplessness, of groping in a thickening fog, of doom, catastrophe and death. We are going to need support, but we can also stay in charge (concerning this seeming paradox, we will have some more to say later). For our support, a growing sense of concern and gratitude will presently come into being. As we come through the experience of surviving doubt and panic in successive nights and days the feeling that we have done it once, so we can do the same again, builds up slowly; step by step we find new confidence. A belief in our inner resources is beginning to take root. This, in turn, instils in us a sense of life instead of death, even if we can accept that ultimately we will die. Going forward from that point, once we can trust experience to intuit deeper meanings, we may perceive that our earlier fears, our loneliness and our despair were not, in truth, concerned with death in its colloquial sense at all. They centred on a different dread, stark and archaic as it is, namely of abandonment, which underlies the fear of death, though deeply buried within most of us. This is a primal terror: that we have been left, cast aside to fall apart or peter out by a bad, uncaring mother, before our life could claim to have begun.

Terrors like this can cut us off from experiencing *experience*, from intimacy with ourselves on which the communion with others, that gives life its deeper meaning and depth and colour to our aims, will invariably depend. The fear that everything may fall apart, that 'all the king's horses and all the king's men' will never put us together again, once we have fallen off the wall, or that in W.B. Yeats' lines, 'things fall apart, the centre cannot hold', constitutes a legacy from our earliest infant days. Where it remains unmodified, we suffer persecutory dread which makes such a misery of life that some can be driven to suicide.

What we have just sketched here is a basic ABC of the development of the earliest infant mind as we understand it now; this will be our subject for the remainder of this chapter.

During the half century which Freud devoted, as we saw, to charting the unconscious mind with its complex processes and structure, he repeatedly paused to question what was going on in the deeper mind of children. What he found often verified theoretical conclusions based on findings in his work with adults.

The famous case of Little Hans is a charming illustration. Following his sister's birth, this lively little boy developed such a phobia of horses that he could no longer leave the house for walks or play as previously, since this meant encountering these work-a-day quadrupeds, drawing loads and carriages. The father, supervised by Freud, slowly learnt to listen in to the boy's phantasies, which centred on anxieties of how and where this new baby came from; the little sister who had no 'widdler' like himself or the great, big horses which the child had studied in the street. As these communications were deciphered, gradually, over several months, so the symptoms disappeared and did not return again. Unlike the dissident Jung, who was pursuing similar paths to chart the unconscious mind, Freud remained fascinated by small children and observed them carefully. It was a baby in a cot, playing with a cotton reel, who drew his attention to the basis of anxiety stemming from a mother's absence. With this, the ground had been prepared for the discoveries which followed.

If Freud's observations and the feat of his self-analysis had mapped the mind's development to the age of three or four, the question still remained unanswered, in any satisfactory manner, as to what had gone before. The theory of infantile sexuality still left conspicuous blanks as to development during the earliest months and years. Infants were thought to be entirely wrapped up in themselves, in a state of so-called auto-eroticism, until, it appeared, they sprang to life into the passionate furore of the Oedipal commotion; babies were little sleeping beauties who somehow from one day to the next erupted into baffling passions to wrest a father or a mother to fill their own romantic needs.

To this day there is no shortage of support for these beliefs. However, in the early 1920s, Melanie Klein, a follower of Freud and herself a mother of three children, was to show with great conviction that the discoveries of Freud had a whole pre-history of far-reaching significance. Encouraged by her colleagues and her second Freudian analyst, Karl Abraham, in Berlin, a leading follower of Freud, she began to analyse children as young as three and four who were seriously disturbed. It was never her intention to start a Kleinian School, even when she came to England, later in that same decade. She adhered most strictly to the methodology of Freud but replaced the previous verbal free association with the play and chatter of the child lost in a world of phantasy. She provided little toys. There were Mummy, Daddy and Baby dolls, sand and water, paper, and glue – whatever children might require to express their phantasies through the medium of play. Naturally, she drew the line at patient or therapist getting hurt, but short of that anything went during the session, which she retained as the classical period of 50 minutes. She watched and listened carefully while she participated in the play, and drew conclusions faithfully from that material day by day. What followed through the months and years would prove to be a major breakthrough which Freud himself had all but broached in the case of Little Hans. Mrs Klein was, as we know not the only psychoanalyst who was treating young children. But the decisive difference in technique as in results was that she worked fully with the negative transference, unlike Anna Freud. This meant that deep anxieties rooted in sadism and in the aggressive instincts could begin to surface and to be contained, so that her patients often showed rapid clinical improvement which tended to endure.

What had prevented Freud from grasping the full implications when Little Hans spoke of the 'stork box' in which his little sister came? When, in his vivid phantasies, the child returned time and again to his anxious preoccupations with the inside of mother's body and everything that happened there? What might possibly have been the nature of this startling block in Freud's developing thought? Did Freud as a man, at the deepest level still shrink back from seeming foolish if he, himself, directly paid continuous attention and respect to the prattle of small children, in his solemn working day, in the way a mother can? As a clinician, Freud could be wonderfully free, at ease to loop the loop of fantasy. When he sat down at his desk, however, he closed those gates to some extent and tried to be respectable in some compartment of his mind. Maybe he was too afraid of his own femininity and needed to stand some common ground with all the other clever men who held office at the time. He was, after all, a Herr Professor with everything this implied for such a conscientious man. Even genius still inhabits a human being subject to contemporary fads and foibles which hedge it in in various ways. Besides, the harvest Freud had sown could not possibly be reaped within a single, human lifespan, and it was for his followers to labour in those fields which are still waiting to be gleaned.

Mrs Klein saw herself as a thresher of that corn. Many aspects of her life, her origins and her own times, delayed her arrival at her full creative potential until the second half of her life. It would, I think, be fair to say that it was the furore her discoveries aroused which drove her to the realization of her originality. Almost against her will, she was driven to see her observations and the concepts to which they had given life and form, as differing from some of Freud's in respects which would have far-reaching consequences both for theory and technique. As the attacks continued to reach a crescendo from many quarters in the ranks, a certain streak of the virago was drawn and dragged to the fore to defend her life's work, as a mother will her child when its survival is threatened. The tempestuous temperament of this woman of genius, together with her ideas, drew the world's hostility into a single vortex, as had been the case with Freud's theories. Many of her contemporaries turned a blind or envious eye until truth with her own hands took the bandages away; so that the value of her work came to be appreciated increasingly throughout the world.

Certainly, after Mrs Klein nothing was the same again; this simple truth speaks for itself. She made it clear, beyond all doubt, from the inception of her work in the 1920s in Berlin, which spanned no less than four decades, that the smallest child could fall victim to neurosis which, in the absence of skilled help, would almost certainly prevent wholesome, sound development towards full maturity and a productive and creative life. Once a new truth comes to light there is no stopping any more. Whatever its gestation time, from the moment labour starts, the contractions do not cease until delivery takes place: and the world acknowledges, at last, that a new idea is born which we had been waiting for. Perhaps we should not be surprised that it was a mother who initiated what would soon be taught as child analysis.

To illustrate one case in point let us meet a little girl who was helped by Mrs Klein, in the therapist's own words:

Erna, a child of six, had a number of severe symptoms. She suffered from sleeplessness, which was caused partly by anxiety in particular by a fear of robbers and burglars and partly by a series of obsessional activities. These consisted in lying on her face and banging her head on the pillow, in making rocking movements . . . in obsessional thumb-sucking and in excessive and compulsive masturbation. All these obsessional activities which prevented her from sleeping at night were carried on in the daytime as well . . . She suffered from severe depressions, which she would describe by saying, 'There's something about life I don't like . . .' She completely dominated her mother, left her no freedom and plagued her continually with her love and hatred.

In Mrs Klein's four volumes of collected work, spanning four decades, there are many 'Little Ernas'; stunted, twisted little minds who hardly see the light of day, in other words reality, since they are so engaged in battle with the demons of their phantasy life. Mrs Klein wrote of little Dick, mute and painfully withdrawn, who around the age of four could hardly say any basic words. He was given two wooden trains. 'Mummy train and Daddy train,' Mrs Klein encouraged him. She writes:

he picked up the train I called 'Dick' and made it roll to the window and said 'station'. I explained, 'the station is Mummy; Dick is going into Mummy'. He left the train, ran into the space between the outer and inner doors of the room, shut himself in, saying 'dark' and ran out again directly. He went through this performance several times.

So Dick's analysis began. 'It had been possible for me, in Dick's analysis,' Mrs Klein writes, 'to gain access to his unconscious by getting in contact with such rudiments of phantasy life and symbol formation as he displayed.' Her paper about Dick was written in 1930; she had already been at work for over a decade by then. So what had been her starting point? From which branch of the Freudian tree had her own thinking taken off, during her second analysis, in Berlin with Abraham?

Freud once observed a boy of some 18 months play the following little game when his mother left the room. With perseverance, again and again he threw a wooden cotton reel over the railings of his cot. 'O-O-o-o', he lamented, meaning gone. Then, by pulling on the cotton, he made the reel reappear again. 'Da!' he repeated gleefully the minute it came back in sight, only to throw it down again and bring it back another time to say 'Da' and drop it yet again. He was, as Freud had understood, attempting to master an event which made him anxious and disturbed – his mother's absence from the room. Rather than suffer it passively he became the master of his fate. 'Da!' he said, and brought her back, radiant with his own success.

Now if a child of 18 months was very obviously at work mastering anxiety with this transparent little game as Freud himself had pointed out, then this anxiety, thought Mrs Klein, must have a pre-history. If Freud had already said that 'the infant cannot as yet distinguish between temporary absence and permanent loss', and this was irrefutable to judge by all the evidence, then what might be the nature of the conflicts generated by this earliest anxiety fuelled by separation? Where, Mrs Klein must have asked herself, did these phenomena begin? Was not anxiety itself the thread to slowly follow back to its very origins? In the consulting room, field of battle that it often was, her troubled little clientele acted out the most bloodcurdling phantasies with murderous intent. They cowered afterwards, terrified, or in remorse expecting doomsday to ensue: an eye for an eye and nothing less. What was the meaning of it all? And what about a child like Dick, who did not show anxiety, who only stood there paralysed and practically mute. What about his anxiety? What was going on in here? Mrs Klein:

The impression his first visit left on me was that his behaviour was quite different from that which we observe in neurotic children. He had let his nurse go without manifesting any emotion and had followed me into the room with complete indifference. There he ran to and fro in an aimless, purposeless way, and several times he also ran round me, just as if I was a piece of furniture . . . The expression of his eyes and face was fixed, faraway and lacking interest. Compare once more the behaviour of children with severe neuroses. I have in mind children who, without actually having an anxiety attack, would on their first visit to me withdraw shyly and stiffly into a corner . . . In all these modes of behaviour the great latent anxiety is unmistakable. The corner or the little table is a place of refuge from me. But Dick's behaviour had no meaning or purpose, nor was any affect or anxiety associated with it.

What was she to make of that? She tells us presently, 'In Dick, there was a complete and apparently constitutional incapacity of the ego to tolerate anxiety'. She explains how in this retarded little boy, phantasies about the damage his genital had done to the inside of 'the station', his mother's body, had brought all phantasy life and symbol formation to an early halt. Terrified of his destructive impulses, he had been unable to progress in his development. Every movement would, he feared, cause destruction followed by retaliation from the dangers deep inside his mother's body into which he had projected his sadistic phantasies. Since every fresh mastery is experienced concretely as seizing something which is new, and so is equated with aggression, he could not even hold a knife or master words with which to speak. Anxiety, that spur to growth in manageable quantities, had been disbanded to be held in what is called the latent state, which happens where a fragile ego cannot deal with it at all.

This anxiety in hiding, not in evidence before, became manifest as soon as Mrs Klein interpreted that the 'station' represented the inside of mother's body. When in response the little patient presently muttered 'dark', she knew that he had understood. The path to his unconscious mind had been located and the access cleared. Symbol formation, halted by such an overload of terror, could begin to go ahead now that there was understanding to offer hope and bring support.

If Charcot and his followers had found themselves mystified by much they witnessed in the Salpêtrière, Melanie Klein now surveyed the decapitated dolls, smashed up little cars and wagons, pools of red paint mixed with glue, and drawings whose content could make one's hair stand on end, with similar bewilderment. Was she not watching, day by day, the enactment of whole crimes demanding new detective work?

Let us pause here, to reflect what intellectual centuries had flown past since Charcot's day whose life had in fact ended a mere three decades before. What a testimony to the strides that genius will take – by which it can be recognized! We need only ask the question: what was happening on that scene before?-to see before our eyes the scale of her contribution.

What conclusions could be drawn from this new detective work concerning the ego's very first phases in development, that central workshop of the mind which relates the Id's unconscious drives to our highest aspirations and maintains a state of truce to include reality? Mrs Klein, of course, was not the only worker in the field to ask herself these questions about the unmapped territory of the rudiments of the Ego during the first months of life. But, certainly, she was the first to pay meticulous attention to the full expression of the aggressive impulses which others found too disturbing to interpret to the child. Since the line of her enquiry followed anxiety back as far as possible, sadism, hatred and aggression, even on a murderous scale, had to be squarely faced if the earliest infant mind was to be comprehended in the full light of day. Just what took place in the beginning, Mrs

Klein now asked herself; much as the Old Testament asks the question, opening with Genesis. Certainly, the first concern had to be with survival, and this could only be maintained, terribly precariously, against that old adversary – annihilation – hour by hour.

If birth is a momentous rally for the mother in each case, then surely, for the neonate it represents little less than absolute catastrophe. To have that safe, warm habitat turn traitor and to be propelled headfirst into the cold, hard light and the raw hands of the air, to have the inflow of supplies from the old friend the placenta cut, from one minute to the next, to have to learn to breathe and suck, to suffer hunger, pain and cold and our other deadly enemies, must surely be the prototype of every dreaded cataclysm in our later phantasy. Now, the only bastion against this persecutory onslaught will surely be the mother's breast. We only have to stop and listen to a newborn baby's cry to tune into the rawest plea to be assisted not to die and perish in a cold unknown, to gauge the baby's expectations. Will not the rescuer and friend have to be ideal and perfect in just every way if it is going to oppose these other deadly enemies crowding in from every side?

Mrs Klein, as we have said, was one of several in this field, all women, struggling to unravel the secrets of the mind's start in life. But she was the only one to believe without a doubt that this earliest Ego was relating closely to the breast, that it was 'object related' from the start. The Ego was not, she found, as other Freudians thought, 'auto-erotic' at this stage, simply wrapped up in itself in complete self-centredness; the theory that it was made a nonsense of all her careful observations, which led her to deduce a passionate relatedness from the very start of life. The problem was to understand the details of its earliest nature. Which factors constituted health and which spelt maldevelopment such as afflicted little Dick and the other troubled children she was seeing day by day? Like Charcot, she surveyed the facts and findings till they formed themselves into patterns in her mind. Her strength, like Charcot's and Freud's lay in an ability to endure prolonged frustration in the face of the unknown and not to feel frightened of the dark. Step by step, she came to see that the children she was treating separated 'good' and 'bad', to keep them very far apart. Sessions tended to begin with a 'bad' Mummy, of whom the child appeared afraid. After a while, she might be 'good' and at the end of the session she would generally turn 'bad' again, above all before separation: the weekend break and holidays. At such times she noticed that this split between good and bad was even more extreme as anxiety ran riot and a really evil witch began to dominate the play. Then, the otherwise 'good' Mummy had to be fantastically good, a veritable Fairy Godmother who would satisfy each wish here and now, this very instant, and not frustrate a single one. At times like that, Mrs Klein recognized how the earlier split would widen into a huge gulf yawning between monster-bad and angel good whenever separation threatened.

From all these observations in Mrs Klein's consulting room, certain conclusions could be drawn as to how the infant related to the very early breast. The breast which was present, which sustained, comforted, warmed and 'understood', was the good breast, at that time. If it was absent it was bad; it brought colic, cold and terror. If frustration was extreme, the breast was diabolical, posing such a fearful threat that the good was idealized as an insurance policy against the danger from the harm that the bad was going to inflict. This ideal breast worked miracles, flowed like a fountain day and night, and never took a moment off to be with father and produce another baby; God forbid! To prevent such a catastrophe, the early Ego in its helplessness believed itself all-powerful, omnipotent in other words. It might in phantasy control every movement of the breast, even in cruel and sadistic ways. It must, at any price, remain in sole possession of this fountainhead. Yet, step by step what became clear was that the infant's inner world was still more complex. For when frustration was running high, when feelings of hatred and of rage which sprang up in consequence and seemed too dangerous to contain, threatened like so much high explosive, this split, as first line of defence was felt to be inadequate. Then the Ego would resort to attempts to rid itself of such persecuting terrors, which felt like death at work within. Calling on omnipotence to deny its helplessness, in this extremis the Ego would say, 'Out with you murderous feelings which are eating me, get out, into the breast out there and keep each other company and leave me safe, please, and in peace'.

That shaky Ego cannot know, in these autocratic tantrums, why such tricks will never work. Desperate to defend itself from the enemy within, in its struggle to survive, it bundles out all knowledge of inner, psychic reality, to find itself left at the mercy of a doubly dangerous breast harbouring its own projections. What is more, this manoeuvre, if it is not modified, undermines the essential, first attempts of integration. The Ego which resorts to it beyond the earliest weeks of life, is weakened as a consequence, while a further mechanism compounds the existing risk. *Projection* only constitutes one direction of a two-way traffic; aspects of the outer world are taken in by *introjection*. This mechanism starts to build and furnish our inner world. Its first inmates, so to speak, will be a good breast and a bad. But if the bad, outer breast is poisoned by attacks and the infant's own projections it will be internalized in a very dangerous form, that of a destructive monster which will lead to fresh denials and further 'splitting', as we say. It is not difficult to see that as a consequence a vicious circle is set up with enemies on every side: a dangerous and hostile world which shows no signs of letting up, and is experienced, in turn, as highly persecutory. This can become the basis for more serious mental illness whose manifestations in this light become comprehensible, in experience as in theory.

Let us return to Mrs Klein. The precarious state of affairs threatening the early Ego is, as we have outlined here, the starting point to every life. Seeing that it is helpful to give phenomena a name, and so have some idea in common regarding basic premises, she called this early state of mind the paranoid-schizoid position, position meaning point in time, a point from which we can move onwards, as we will do presently, but also one we may return to if excessive stress and strain (inner compounded by outer), forces the Ego to retreat back to there in later life.

When such a retreat takes place, which is called a regression, that person is then suffering from a severe degree of illness such as paranoia or schizophrenia. The Infant moving through the paranoid-schizoid position is, of course, not psychotic, or certainly not at this point in time if the breast environment holds the unintegrated fragments of the early infant mind until they start to integrate and come together healthily. Here, a critical distinction between two diverse situations has to be clarified. We must differentiate between primary unintegration held by a containing mother, where everything is going well, and disintegration or falling apart where the task of integration was not accomplished well enough.

What exactly do we mean by this term 'integration'? What is it that must come together, to join up and integrate, to ensure mental health and adequate stability? What we have been looking at is a bleak and threatening scene, a truly blasted inner heath, a landscape like the one described in the opening of *Macbeth*, sinister indeed. Yet infants normally move on to the next 'position' later, during the first year of life. What will bring this change about? What is the nature of its matrix, this advent of an inner climate which is more benevolent? What lessens splitting between 'good' and 'bad', where the breast as 'part object' slowly fades out of the picture while mother comes to be experienced more and more often as a whole? Here, everything still begs the question of what facilitates this change.

The answer is, the mother's function, which a follower of Mrs Klein called maternal reverie. Feeding is a part of it. But over and beyond the feeding is the way a mother's mind can tune into her infant's needs with a sensitivity which peaks in the post-natal months to serve this very crucial purpose. As the milk comes in, so does an influx of this fine maternal sensitivity attuned to the anxieties which her infant will express in a thousand different ways long before he learns to speak. Anxieties in the infant are aroused by the impact of frustration on an organism in a state of abject helplessness. With this twofold sustenance of being fed and understood (the continuous experience of maternal reverie), the belief in the good breast, in the inner and the outer world, is strengthened as the days go by. Frustration grows more tolerable. Hate falls back in the face of love, until Freud's sombre confrontation, the duality of life and death, embarks on a degree of fusion to establish a well-knit mind, even if that fusion cannot ever sew a final seam.

Gradually, where all goes well, where love and care are good enough to keep frustration within bounds, good feelings both of hope and trust may gradually win the day over suspicion and the fear of death and annihilation, which previously was felt to lie in waiting almost hourly: the doomsday feeling which, if unrelieved, some people carry all through life. In such a climate of benevolence, and where the infant's constitution is rich enough in hope and love, a loving breast will be instated in all its radiance in the inner world, to be followed presently by a good mother as a whole.

So far so good, we may well think with a sigh of deep relief. But we are not yet home and dry. For now another fear arrives. If mother is loved so very much and her importance to survival slowly acknowledged in the inner world, feelings of possessiveness and the fear of losing her become fiercely powerful, just when the infant, at this stage, relates not only to his mother's breast but to her body as a whole. Somewhere inside there, he assumes, grow supplies of everything wonderful upon this earth. In there he envisages an ever-flowing paradise to which he certainly intends to be and stay the only heir. Here, infantile omnipotence is heading for a painful fall. Other babies are felt to be growing there, inside, on a sort of baby-tree which produces endless fruit. To make matters even worse, and very threatening indeed, father as a part object, roams around there, cock-a-hoop, feeding on this heavenly food, just as though he owned the place. It follows from these phantasies that an angry baby feels, 'If I'm not having mother now, someone else is having her. It must be father, hateful "thing".' He sees that father is, at first, a part-object too, a penis, until just like with mother's breast, he is experienced as a whole.

What Mrs Klein uncovered here is nothing less than the drama of a whole pre-history to Freud's own foundation stone: infantile sexuality, the Oedipus complex in its fiery nemesis and majesty. 'But how can infants know about a penis, now, for heaven's sake! This is taking things too far', the old chorus in the wings of progress through the centuries strikes up. Yet there are reasons why the infant's mind would contain a preconception of this kind. Even if we leave aside the controversial area of pre-natal apprehension of parental intercourse, the hard long nipple, in the soft, round mouth, and projecting firmly from the soft warm breast provides the earliest fantasies for a 'combined object', foreshadowing the primal scene and food for thought about a penis from our very earliest days of proverbial innocence. (And we will shortly find another, when we glance at Bion's work.) This 'intercourse' is obviously not conceived in adult terms. During this first or 'oral' phase when every satisfaction is still focussed on the infant's mouth, every pleasure on this earth is construed to be a feed. Accordingly, the breast and penis, in the infant's phantasy, get together in the night to feed each other heavenly nectar, while the infant lies alone and rages, hungry, in the dark, if he is lonely and awake while no one comes to comfort him. Because the infant longs to have the nipple always in the mouth, so he assumes this parental feeding carries on uninterrupted. The breast and penis joined together, and subsequently the two parents, combined in sexual intercourse, which the infant will attack sadistically in phantasy, out of his anguish at exclusion, become the terrifying monster of many a small person's nightmares.

These proto-ideas make their appearance when the teeth are being cut, which fact of life exacerbates cannibalistic phantasies with regard to these attacks launched against the sexual parents 'combined against him' in the night. Terror of retaliation is a common cause of nightmares which disrupt the 'teething' nights. Around this time, the scene is set for a momentous change in the infant's inner world. Since splitting with its wild projections is gradually lessening, as part-objects slowly grow into their whole counterparts, the infant starts to apprehend that this 'bad' mother whom he attacks, is the same as the 'good' mother whom he loves and on whose loving his survival must depend. Whereas previously his fear and abject terror centred on the survival of his Ego, they now begin to focus on this actual mother as a whole; on his 'good object,' as we say, both the outer one and the one enshrined in his inner world.

While this shift is taking place and ambivalence is lessening, his manifold anxieties that his attacks may damage his mother beyond his powers of repair bring feelings of depression on. After the first six months of life, a capacity for concern, and in its wake for deep remorse, is starting to manifest itself. The object is no longer exploited in a greedy, ruthless way for everything it has to give, at all hours of the day and night, and then used as a dumping ground for fears and terrors of all kind – a 'toilet-breast' as we say, which will sluice away projection; but it is also cherished for its life and love-giving qualities. In other words, an early wish to take responsibility for the wellbeing of mother, which gradually extends to others, is very slowly setting in among the manifold relapses and the sorrows of remorse.

The pain of causing so much hurt to somebody we also love, as part of our predicament, is beginning to be faced and shouldered as a lifelong task – the task of human sanity. This momentous starting point towards eventual mental health, which features periods of depression, even at this earliest age, Mrs Klein duly named the 'depressive position'. Its arrival, as she found, heralds new integration and growing strength within the Ego, from before the age of one, within a deepening acceptance of the great importance of our inner, or, psychic reality. But like every new step forward this achievement also carries with it dangers of relapse. Where hatred and destructive feelings run particularly fierce, either constitutionally or due to environmental failure, pain and remorse may be so strong, beyond endurance, possibly, that a back-sliding takes place to that earlier status quo where this turmoil is split off and projected, as before. If this happens, it grew clear in the work of Mrs Klein, complications lie in wait. For whenever we project parts of our mind or feelings, or our personality, which we would rather not contain, into another person then, by a process which she called projective identification, we attack those aspects in that other person which account for our more irrational hates.

The same applies in the reverse. We may split our good parts off, in case our destructive feelings overwhelm or damage them, and then love the recipient equally absurdly too; or we may fear we have no loving feelings. The more we carry on like this, the weaker will our Ego be, the more precarious and at risk of splitting up and fragmenting it will be when psychosis supervenes.

If this bare outline has presented these formidable dynamics as cut and dried, in their succession, this is not the case in life where there is always flux and flow, regression and progression too, a constant two-way traffic. But where development goes forward the depressive position will, despite setbacks now and then, be progressively worked through until here, too, a second time, love and life are well enough in the ascendancy to regain a reasonable degree of stability. Even so, the story of Job always serves as a reminder that where we are sorely tried, the most secure among us may begin to falter and show cracks.

Suffering and human loss try our fortitude at every turn. Ill health, poverty and death lie in wait for all of us. There are disasters that nature springs on us, and those we bring upon ourselves. Prisons and concentration camps, totalitarian regimes, governments who do not care for the underprivileged, loneliness in our old age, how countless are the hidden traps strewn along our human path. We are rarely home and dry. Backsliding or regressions can be the fate of all of us. The Gospels tell of how unresolved was the outcome for Jesus Christ. Those four historians disagree. They all acknowledge that Christ cried out before giving up the ghost: 'Father, into thy hands I commend my spirit' and, 'God, my God, why hast thou forsaken me?' But they fail to reach consensus on which of these cries He uttered, significant as this is.

Was Christ's Object 'good' or 'bad' before he actually died? The Gospels leave us in the dark. Matthew and Luke disagree and Mark and John remain obscure. Like Mrs Klein, the Gospels say there is no knowing until the very end whether we can keep our hold on our good object in the inmost heart when the winds of fate ride high and hatred converges from all sides.

This is the issue which underlies human drama, great and small. Here it is that we hold our breath and have to sit and sweat it out. This is the crux of mental health in terms of our development, where each must fight the battle out with as much responsibility as he can muster, with support. Here, ultimately we fall or stand. This is the achievement which, even if we do not know it, each expects of himself. And each will in his heart of hearts review the balance sheet of progress at intervals throughout his life.

If we now look at this within the wider context of our central argument; where someone wants to abdicate from this momentous undertaking, he has the right to make that choice. But we as doctors cannot choose and decide for our patients. We have to say, to each 'Fight on. Try to understand yourself. Be more than human, if you like, but do not opt for being less, and we will help you bear the pain for we cannot grow upright and strong and good and straight, as sane as possible in every case, without facing conflict and enduring pain'. Now such an attitude demands the very most from each of us. It is easier to put an honest combatant to sleep than to hear the noise of battle rage. But there is time enough to sleep when we are actually dead. Life is a time to be awake. It is because we know these truths deeply, in our inmost mind, even if we hide them from ourselves, that society remains opposed to the abuse of alcohol and drugs. People will resort to these when they cannot bear their psychic pain or stand their inner reality. Seen in developmental terms, why we fall victim to all means that promise us forgetfulness, is not hard to understand. Yet these crutches and these aids are not easily withdrawn without psychotherapy.

As long as we oppose the use of illicit drugs, the same reasoning must apply to those which we prescribe as well. Their use can never be ruled out. People when they are disturbed can be very violent, dangerous to others and themselves. To deny this is to fly in the face of all reality, which no doctor ought to do. But to dish them out for our own convenience or for that of relatives may not be permissible, on more detailed scrutiny. And such scrutiny ought perhaps to be instituted now that we are growing more aware that many of these drugs cause harm and many of them cause addiction. They will confiscate a life instead of augmenting it, as the purveyors claim. They, we must remember are guided by the profit motive, one which should have no place in these profound considerations.

Leaving these matters to one side for a moment, we are not yet at the end of this basic ABC without a mention of the work of Bion, who was influenced by Freud and the work of Mrs Klein.

To get to grips with Bion proves an intimidating task. His was a mind which was at home in higher mathematics, history and philosophy, as in his chosen field of work he had slowly moved towards in a rich and varied life, namely depth psychology. Today, the mountain of his thought draws ever more expeditions by psychotherapists. And since it throws new beams of light on our fundamental sanity, let us take binoculars and cast a tantalizing look at the rock face from a distance.

From which branch of knowledge, of the growing Freudian tree, did this psychoanalyst come? The answer is that he took his starting point from Mrs Klein's concept of projective identification, the pushing of contents of our mind into others, who are then either attacked or idealized. Mrs Klein's ideas were first set out in a paper which she called 'Notes on Some Schizoid Mechanisms', published in 1946. Her editors refer to it as 'the first map of a region before known only in general outline; much remains to be filled in'. Bion initially set out on this task of filling in. But he accomplished more than that. Mrs Klein's map enabled Bion and several other followers to begin treating schizophrenic patients or make some sense of those in treatment, while adhering closely to the method which Freud laid down without pragmatic deviations. It was, with this fidelity, regardless of the difficulties, amply strewn along the way, that Klein's followers differed from other psychoanalysts who approached that frozen world elsewhere in the post-war era, like Fromm-Reichman and Stack Sullivan. The schizophrenic patients whom these analysts began to treat were erupting into words which did not communicate, in the ordinary sense, anything about themselves their fellow human beings could understand, with the best will in the world. What textbooks of psychiatry and most psychiatrists today call 'thought disorder' added up to little more than gibberish, as any listener can confirm who has struggled to decode the tantalizing jigsaw talk of the schizophrenic patient. What is more, it frightens one, as can be the case with dreams. To sit and listen to this talk, or rather effluence, by the hour demands the utmost fortitude, since it expresses hinterlands which we have thankfully outgrown and severed all connections with, so that we may function in the world and accomplish adult tasks with a sufficiency of love, wholeness and belief in life.

Whether frightening or not, this is what Wilfred Bion did, just as did the other analysts who brought Kleinian ideas to bear upon the no man's land before them. The question which confronted Bion, that seemed to stare him in the ears, to think a Bion line of thought, was very simply, what is thought? How exactly do we think? Does thinking generate our thoughts or are there thoughts which we then think? Neither Freud nor Mrs Klein had as yet conceptualized this uncharted territory. The task dictated a focus on phenomena which implied that a patient's mind destroyed its own capacity for thought for reasons which had to be explained by underlying phantasy. From observations that Bion made in his own consulting room, it gradually grew clear to him that his patients in their minds were making an attack on links. From the infantile attack on parental intercourse, where the penis is a link, from an attack upon the breast which links the mother to her child through the nipple between breast and mouth, these schizophrenics began to attack all the crucial links which bind verbal intercourse and thereby those conjunctions upon which symbol formation must depend. Absent symbols in their turn mean that words are used as things arising out of concrete thought. Furthermore, as Bion found, functions become things as well.

Because this cut schizophrenics off from life, these patients started hating life in all its aspects, meaning thought, emotion, creativity, all that binds parts into a unity. Since they destroyed their access to ordinary human life they attacked and envied our precious, common human ground with its joy and with its pain, and above all its frustrations, which these patients could not stand. All of this they would replace with a silent, frozen ecstasy or with grandiosity as a defence against despair like the patient who arrived and said 'I am not made of wood' (Foudraine, 1971). Nevertheless these states of mind, unlike what Freud himself believed, were peopled very vividly with part and primitive whole objects, a shifting phantasmagoria in which these sufferers were absorbed to the exclusion of all else. When internal war broke out, these patients would become disturbed, since these inner battlefields would be envisaged in the outer world. The confused perceptions which resulted, and the inner debris of all sorts, might be evacuated as hallucinations now and then, using the body's musculature or the sense organs in reverse, like the alimentary system. Just as one function of the dream is to preserve the dreamer's sleep, so hallucinations serve to preserve that state of mind which is like a waxwork gallery where gruesome models wake and sleep, come to life and come to death in disturbing sequences. In order to accommodate these baffling phenomena, gleaned in the consulting room during several years of work, Bion generated two 'empty' concepts which he called Alpha function and Beta elements.

Perceptions, whether they derive from sense impressions of the outer world or emotional experience, have, he suggested, to be worked on by Alpha function; they are either stored as memories or used as thoughts (which lead to thinking) or they are used as dreams for dreaming in the night. If not digested in this manner for these creative purposes, Beta elements remain. These cannot be used for thoughts in our waking experience, or for dreams, or stored away as memory to build into experience, from which we otherwise could learn. They are a debris which either clogs or rumbles round in mental space, rather, I imagine, like hardware junk in outer space which is not brought back to earth. Alternatively, the mind at certain intervals, as Bion the clinician showed us, has a motion like the bowels; evacuates this content with a grimace or a twist of the features or the limbs, a muscle-language: gibberish, from which a great deal can be learned.

I used to watch a schizophrenic in a blue macintosh plod uphill with the strangest, leaning-forward sort of gait, highly evocative of something I could not put a finger on until it struck me, after several weeks, that he was identifying himself with Nanny-pushing-him-in-pram. When Alpha function penetrates the bog of Beta elements, then the basic prototype of every intercourse takes place. This is the further reason why an infant would already 'know' that such an intercourse exists from the personal experience of his mother's understanding reaching through the wastes of panic to mobilize his Alpha function and thereby his sanity.

What is the nature of this function of maternal reverie, linked to Bion's other concept of the container and contained? The infant, as we saw before, projects his fear of dying and various other terrors and frustrations, into the maternal breast. A mother who is 'good enough' contains the unintegrated Ego and accepts this stream of debris and the projections it will emit, to return them by and by 'predigested' and detoxified. The infant, in his basic dread of falling to bits or falling out of life, can begin to feel contained in this pre-verbal two-way flow across a membrane or a barrier as it will in time become, between conscious and unconscious content. In mental health, the barrier maintains optimal permeability in two directions, as before.

For a mother to put her capacity for Alpha function at her little one's disposal in this timeless way, until he is able to start developing his own, is an exhausting task for all its day-by-day rewards. During this period, she should feel able to rely upon a steady flow of support from her partner, her relatives, her friends and from society at large which, if it is good enough will hold provision in the wings for various contingencies, considering what is at stake. Here lies the deepest reason for maintaining a tradition of two-parent families. There is a body of opinion in certain feminist circles which tends to spurn and to deride this time-honoured norm today, at considerable risk to the new generation. For this is where the father's role approaches sheer necessity, not only as a 'hunter', or breadwinner, as we say, but for this specialized support as auxiliary container, to help the mother's mind to process her infant's projections on demand until they lessen by and by and life, once more, returns to normal. Where, for any one of countless reasons, this maternal function, in relation to her infant's needs fails, his mind may lack strong foundations for emotional and intellectual growth. This may stay hidden for some time. Difficulties are put down to the fact that 'he is still only a child' which, of course is often true. It may require expert help to seek to differentiate something which is sinister from a passing phase.

Couched in our current language, these concepts embody truths known to mothers through the ages, in hovels, palaces and tents. Bion said that only lies need a thinker, that the truth lies ready waiting to be found; his originality of mind encompassed many fields and areas. A truth, once it has been found, starts to spread across the earth, as a relay marathon where the torch is handed on. Freud, Abraham, Klein and Bion have between them carried it through an entire century. This means that we can now understand something we have always 'known', that a mother's reverie is the very matrix of the cornerstone of sanity. This truth will never go away. These events within the mind, which have just been outlined here, point out new directions now. They confront us irrefutably. Massive ignorance remains. This is not under dispute. But what we cannot afford is the purveyor of ignorance in a post of human trust. That is less than 'good enough' when a sufferer in quest of help is confounded in his search, when he is side-tracked and confused and thrown back on his inner dark. Truth, as everybody knows is never short of enemies, since it brings about change. Change we deeply mistrust since it requires adaptation and may stir painful memories belonging to our infancy (which we will return to later). Can we understand their stance, on so many different levels for only understanding helps. Attacks as a rule attract a counter-offensive on the spot. This basic law of tit-for-tat Jesus had understood. 'You have heard it said an eye for an eye and a tooth for a tooth, but I say to you that you resist not evil.' What did Jesus mean by those rather enigmatic words? On reflection, I believe he meant that if you love the good you only work with it in sight. For if you stoop to untrue ways then you also get clogged up with those Beta elements. Alpha function is required to propagate the paths of truth. Jesus, we could say today, spread Alpha function with his words. It brought the opposition out, as it brings it out today. Why this opposition still?

4

The Opposition's Case

In Mary Webb's novel *Gone to Earth* (1917) the protagonist Hazel's brief and vibrant life is dedicated to her pet fox. Both are creatures of the wild: impetuous and unrestrained. Neither of them proves a match for a self-righteous, cruel world, where untamed and passionate beings must be trampled underfoot before their lives have even properly begun. It is the hunt that kills them both when Foxy, foaming-wild with fear, leaps into Hazel's frantic arms as the hounds are closing in. Slowly, as the tale unfolds, in the tangle of the woods, we learn to sniff with their sharp senses for scents of danger on the wind, where they quiver in their fallow, hidden in the wild Welsh hills, sharing joy and ancient fears.

Psychotherapists must live a bit like Hazel and her warm, red fox. They too will learn to sniff the wind for the baying of the hunt on a clear and perfect morning, to bristle at the whiff of hounds and recognize the tooth and tongue ever ready for the kill, even if this hue and cry turns out to be disguised most frequently behind threadbare rationalization or obscure academic jargon. Why, as we go quietly about our private working life, should the followers of Freud, and more so of Klein and Bion, still be persecuted in this way and have to suffer in this manner? What aspect of their undertaking brings the opposition out in force, the full hunt at the break of day?

Effective psychotherapy is concerned with transformation. During this rigorous one-to-one scrutiny through the years, one partner's mind will be leavened. To some extent, and gradually, the heavy dough of wrong assumptions, and myths and barricades will grow lighter, even airy, by virtue of its penetration by the other partner's mind. Sooner or later, the proceedings will assume the character of a grave and joyful dance, once changes in the inner world provide a sense of deeper purpose where hopelessness prevailed before, of openness where all was closed. This penetration is achieved by what we call interpretations, a word which tends to be surrounded by superfluous mystery although it is relatively simple. Verbal intervention will slowly ripen and take shape as the therapist picks up a pattern of unwholesome content within the free associations, where distortions from the past, rekindled in the here and now, have surfaced in the transference to be illuminated. The therapist will then strive to formulate, providing that this content holds sufficient elements of truth, assembled in a manner where they may prove digestible. A certain depth charge is laid. This may home immediately to its unconscious target. Others have to bide their time sometimes over days or years. But as the process finds its pace along these indicated lines, transformation will begin in terms of far-reaching changes in the personality.

Now why, one asks, should this endeavour evoke ferocious opposition in so many other minds, usually uninvolved and on the sidelines? Why should onlookers at large volunteer so much derision and supreme hostility – those who are otherwise indifferent to the toiling of the soul. After all, acupuncture, hypnotism, faith healing, spiritualism, clairvoyance, religion, even human torture hardly draw such concentrated hatred as the quiet, workaday task of the psychotherapist. What elements in this transaction draw this virulent response? Do its practitioners make a claim which is harmful or dishonest? Or is it that they make no claim in the usual, concrete sense of modern sales talk?

'They'll never prove that "it" works.' 'People get better anyway'; psychologists and statisticians join force, heatedly and repeatedly. '*We* can prove there is no case for psycho-analysis', they proclaim at intervals. Let us not be drawn into carrying the bogus weapon of so-called 'evidence' or 'proof', since this kind of duelling must ultimately raise a laugh. Neither party will drop dead. The episode may resemble the tragi-comical encounter between Pierre and Dholokov which Tolstoi described in *War and Peace* over Natasha's honour. Both continue on their way, and certainly no transformation has occurred in consequence, for the ground of the objections lies at a much deeper level than the words themselves suggest. Instead, let me illustrate from personal experience, aspects of this opposition as I have encountered it in the course of daily work, both from onlookers and from patients, since neither party is immune, for all of us mistrust the new for reasons which have been suggested in connection with change.

Several years ago, I worked in a large mental hospital. We ran a little unit housed in a separate bungalow, which was the sole concession to the twentieth century and Freud. The rest, with its 2000 beds, locked wards and padded cells, continued earlier practices which have been touched on earlier. Our unit had some thirty beds. Two or three times every year, rumours reached us from the main building some few hundred yards away that we were going to be closed down. The beds were needed, it was claimed, for rather better purposes. I still remember, vividly, how our poor consultant had at intervals to appear in his best clothes, like a mother under attack for her rumbustious family, and restate the same old case before whatever powers sat on the committee at the time. Around lunch time he returned with the usual reprieve. The committee had no choice. A regulation had appeared, from beyond us and on high, that where any hospital served the purposes of teaching, lip service had to be paid to psychotherapy in terms of a few dozen beds. That latest dictum, issued by the Royal College of Psychiatry, had come in time to spread its wings like a guardian angel over the work we did from day to day. The committee, nonetheless, left us in no uncertainty that our own activities constituted an affront to them which they could not specify. And when occasion took us over into the main hospital, for routine discussion with our colleagues, the corridors seemed booby-trapped, not only in imagination. We were a leper colony and this unhappy response was extended to our patients, who found themselves the object of hatred among other inmates, where envy played no little part. We ourselves were in no doubt that our work represented change; in other words, things to come which might disrupt things as they were and as they had been down the cosy years.

While these skirmishes ran high, my attention focused on an everyday phenomenon which was attacking the task in hand, this time, from among the patients. The patients in our unit were divided into several groups which met three times every week for intensive psychotherapy. These patients were severely ill. Some were psychotic and the rest were what is known as 'borderline', meaning that their sanity was precariously maintained. As the work became routine, so that I began to use my observations more creatively, I focused on the following: every time I introduced a new concept to my group, I had a feeling that it was spat straight back into my face. The experience disconcerted me. The group would do this as a whole. First, perhaps, they fell asleep, which was perfectly routine. When exchanges would resume, they ignored the point I had made; when I brought them back to it, the topic focused on some food which everybody there disliked, or maybe onto being sick if something disagreed with you. Situations of this kind where the members of a group collude at an unconscious level to launch into a joint attack are, of course, the very substance of group psychotherapy.

All this puzzled me at first. I was new still to the job and therefore lacked experiences but I was prepared to wait for further clues to emerge. Bit by bit it dawned on me that these new ideas I brought were experienced like lumps in a substance which was soft and smooth and normally went flowing down in a pleasurable way. One day I put this to the group. They all woke up and agreed. Lumps they were, and horrible; they wanted to spit them out.

I then remembered gradually how my own babies had disliked their first taste of solid food, how each of them screwed up his face and made such heavy weather of it that it was enough to make one weep, for this was about being weaned: lumps appearing in the food. 'Something new' means *no more breast.* Weaning let us here repeat, is the crucial trauma the infant must negotiate on the path to mental health. Every loss in later life will always re-awaken the supreme anxieties of weaning, as Mrs Klein confirmed Freud's earlier discovery. The unfamiliar is the threat which looms above all other threats. It spells the end of paradise. The angel with the flaming sword bars our longing to return to whatever went before, with its familiar consolations.

At the root of these illustrations lie two reasons, I believe, for the hostile opposition to Freud's original ideas and their evolution since. Firstly, we respond to change with such suspicion and hostility because it stands for being weaned; by that token, it represents all the adaptational demands which were briefly mentioned at the end of the previous chapter. The flow of the familiar milk is spoilt with nasty, solid lumps which are often introduced more or less around the time when mother's tummy also turns lumpy with another baby, leaving less room on the lap we had assumed was ours for good. So deeply rooted in our infancy is this outrage and revulsion, that even within Freudian ranks, opposition to new ideas tends to be as virulent as that which meets them from outside; we are quite familiar with this in the history of ideas in a general, wider context. Secondly, ideas begin with Alpha function as we all once imbibed it at the breast. Those who 'have' the ideas, who produce significant and new contributions, had a 'better breast' than we, the infant in us will insist. And so ideas will get attacked because they mean a favoured child. Freud himself always claimed that a mother's oldest child, his own place in the family, – and at the time he still said son – will go into the wider world as something of a conqueror. The firstborn baby gets the cream. So envy plays a leading part in our attack on new ideas. But in the case of Freud's ideas, and the new ones which evolved to cause such fracas in the ranks, we come up against a quite specific cause for virulence. For unlike ideas which spring from impersonal disciplines which can be thought and known 'about', those of depth psychology have, in time, to 'become', if they are to be of help. Their concern is with transformation rather than an empty intellectual task, while some who feel reluctant to enter this experience fend their own frustration off by going into the attack, as in the next illustration.

I had joined the department in a teaching hospital as a psychotherapist, at a time when I was still anything but worldly-wise. A consultant psychiatrist who was shortly to retire and whom I had not yet met sent me a patient to assess, who was terribly deprived. Clearly, as a little boy, he had been almost motherless, although his mother had been around. I set this out in simple terms in my report to him which could have broken any heart. I added words to the effect that the baby part of him had remained so inconsolable that his treatment would imply severe regression, possibly.

Very shortly after that, a social function came around. I took the opportunity to locate this same colleague, this senior psychiatrist, and introduced myself to him. 'Kleinian female, please get out,' he shouted at me angrily. I thought there must be some mistake and shortly, when he reappeared, I said so in all innocence. This time he pushed me very hard, with both hands, fully in the breast, and ran off like a

frightened child, while I burst into floods of tears. Presently, I understood that this happening offered me some important food for thought. As my injured feelings cleared, it became quite obvious that here was not a 'baddy' but a very complicated man. Some years later, when my colleague died, the department went into the deepest mourning of its kind. Social workers, secretaries and nurses stood around and wept. I was taken by surprise, since I had avoided all contact with him from that night. True, I had in fact received a letter of apology but missed the opportunity to enter into dialogue, which I regretted afterwards (as is frequently the case when we stay on our high horse of injured vanity and pride).

Further enquiries which I made after his death revealed a very different man, a man who cared so deeply about the welfare of his patients that he must have worked in great despair, for the most part of his life. At the deepest source it seems that he was painfully aware that he lacked the healing manna of psychoanalysis which he craved but also hated, only to attack it in my person. The little boy whom I described in the reply I sent to him was, I understood, himself. I had touched a hidden spring. The push he gave me, was, I knew, this small boy's appeal for help, perhaps the nearest he had ever come to any such acknowledgement that he also needed help; and I had been deaf and blind to this because of narcissistic hurt. There is, of course, no knowing whether, given a different response, he would have been in a position to meet it in a friendly way.

Educated individuals, as we assume that doctors are, have become pretty expert at learning lots of facts by heart. Yet even if we can read and study Freud, Klein or Bion, as many others on the subject it will not take us very far. Freud himself had to resort to self-analysis before *he* grew to be the path which was leading him. Until that moment, he had stayed on the surface, even though he knew 'about' the unconscious. Only when he sank that shaft of intellectual knowledge into his own unconscious mind did he encounter phantasy and infantile sexuality as his own reality.

The hostility which depth psychology encounters lies deep in the distress of our good psychiatrist rooted in our deeper knowledge, that we remain as we are, with all the suffering implied, or 'become' something else with the help of another human being and the confession this requires that in our naked human essence all of us need support from others throughout life, failing which we stay apart as sufferers and isolates. In other words we will remain trapped in the coils of our neurosis, if we are so afflicted, without psychotherapeutic help. And yet we know in our unconscious, as poets through the ages have, that we all face the world with unfinished baby business rampaging in the deeper mind, demanding to be sorted out if we are to know the joy of maturing into adults, which surely underlies the present growth of psychotherapy.

This baby wants to understand why he had to give up the breast, what was 'wrong' with him that 'they' wanted others after him, or before him as the case may be. Why wasn't he 'good enough'? The adult person wants to know why he reacts the way he does to the others in his life, why his feelings tend to be so irrational at times, why he fights with individuals who represent younger siblings. Why does he hate authority, father figures and the boss? Why does he fear them? What is wrong when he's a mild and decent chap, as he can sense at intervals? His reactions cripple him, to varying degrees, which are minimal at times as in other individuals who may not require help.

But there are some who will always deny the trouble they are in. Then they will attack the very thing which sets their frustrated longing up to add to their other miseries. These are individuals who have to deny their deepest needs, above all for dependency. They are the people who insist, 'I can manage on my own. There is nothing wrong with me. I am not a helpless infant, but can handle this myself just as I have always done.' To such people, needing help evokes the great anxiety of their deeper helplessness, which they continue to deny. They want so badly to be carried, and to be taken in, that any offer of support is felt as a tremendous threat to their selfhood and autonomy. A person who has never yet arrived at experiencing himself as subject fears that he will be taken over in any close relationship, excepting where he is 'the strong one', for all relationships are seen in terms of who is strong or weak, infant or adult, mouth or breast. Besides, how shall he trust another if he has not ever learnt to trust anyone at all? How is he to make demands if he has spent a lifetime burying his basic needs? How is he to place his life in other human hands when that other 'only wants money or kudos', as he will think when he projects his own materialistic thinking. How is he to utilize this new form of nourishment if he is so envious of the provider that he spoils this food with envious attacks until it is felt to poison him? How is he going to remove all this debris from the path to even 'start' on therapy, long before he understands that these preambles, as he supposed, *are* the psychotherapy. Once these obstacles are cleared, and the doubts and suspicions are laid to rest so that he can start to draw close to this other, he is practically there. He is almost home and dry. From there, he can come romping home into the arms he could not see were there, wide open, from the start.

Experiences so profound, issues of such human depth, when they have to be denied as part and parcel of our innermost reality, are converted into hatred of understanding and of help. For all these reasons, many hate this help that tantalizes them because it seems unattainable, generally for inner reasons which they then externalize to convert these sour grapes into so-called 'arguments' of the all familiar kind: 'Neurosis tends to cure itself', or 'The cure is worse than the disease', or 'It's self-indulgence, nothing else.'

'Whoever has that kind of money' is something which we often hear, thrown out with great hostility. Payment can mean to sufferers that they are not really loved, not wanted truly for themselves. We hear this from the very rich, from an alcoholic who spends twice as much on drink or from a drug addict on drugs. We hear it from the wretched miser whose money lies rotting in the bank because he cannot bring himself to spend one penny on himself. But all are haunted by the fear that an investment in themselves may bring nothing in return. Such is the experience of the outer world so far. Why should it turn out to be different now?

Time, and the lack of it, is the other argument which is all too often used. 'This business will go on for years', is something which we tend to hear as a first line of attack. So, of course, does a human life. If a happy life seems all too short, a sufferer and his witnesses experience life as a sentence, endless in its misery. Death to those who are alive is no haphazard accident. It sets a seal on their achievement in terms of love and work and growth, in terms of harvest, fruit and seed. It brings an acquiescence that the time has come to take our leave, however painful this may be. But there is another death which continues throughout life. These living dead live on and on, past rhyme or reason, past the end, like a wintry cabbage patch which nobody has dug up once the gardener went away. A life become a wilderness is bound to take its time to clear. Every gardener will know how many seasons it can take to enrich impoverished soil before anything can grow. In psychotherapy as well, compost has to be dug in, patiently, for many months, before seed falls on growing ground. In many cases, it is worse. A wall of thistles must be cleared or there are dead or dying stumps which have slowly to be eased out, first of all.

But what is the alternative? 'Make the best of a bad job?' 'Get on with it, like all of us?' 'Pull your socks up and don't be daft. 'That is the common repertoire which we are familiar with, and variations on the theme. It is not a pretty one, especially since in every case there is not only this single but many human lives involved. The way in which we live our life has a far-reaching effect, whether we acknowledge it or not. Nobody is an island. Every sufferer sets up a fellowship of suffering. His projections and his envy, his hatred of emotions and of life poison everyone around, as we all have cause to know, while a life which flows at peace spreads ripples of benevolence.

Where is all this leading us? All of us would rather not have our own ideas opposed. Dialectics make us work when we are tempted to be lazy. So why not have an opposition? These opposers are as entitled to their views as we feel we are to ours. But there is one peculiar difficulty confronting us in this approach. We have already touched on it in pointing out the attitude of the patients in the unit who spat interpretations out when they were unfamiliar. The opposition in this case is not 'some other side, out there', it lies entrenched in each of us as the great duality between the two opposing instincts of life and death respectively. Here is a specific pitfall in every human dialogue. We may ask for 'evidence' or 'proof' that this or that is of value, but does the question truly carry genuine human enquiry or is it chosen as a tactic by a cynic or a pragmatist? Which is a policy for life, and which is a stampede for death? How do we tell the two apart, when arguments on either side carry some plausibility? Let us go a little further before returning to this point with its far-reaching implications.

What exactly does it mean to say that we are, all of us, members of the opposition? Does this only apply to 'patients' or each and every one? In people we call patients, the opposition is sometimes easier to observe. Hanna Green's book, *I Never Promised You a Rose Garden*, tells how a young schizophrenic, together with her therapist who was Frieda Fromm-Reichman, worked to break the stranglehold of this crippling form of illness. The patient, who at the time was in a mental hospital, has since become a well-known writer. Here, she tells us how each time that part of her personality which was most seriously afflicted took the smallest step forward, the ill part threatened a fresh attack. 'All of this will lead you nowhere. You were better off before. Take my word, go back to sleep.' If these seductive overtures failed to make the intended impact with their ancient sirens' song, that she was happier asleep, withdrawn from all reality with its troublesome travail, the mind resorted to terrorist tactics in order to enforce submission to the earlier status quo of madness, hatred and suspicion. In other words she had a relapse into madness once again. This backsliding goes by the name of a 'negative therapeutic reaction', also known as N.T.R. This patient would become disturbed, terrified and violent as her fragmented mind became a fearsome inner battleground between sanity and madness, going forward or going back. The two run closely side by side in every psychotherapy. It is one reason why the time for treatment tends to be so long. But we have to bear in mind that not only the schizophrenic goes backtracking in this way. It happens to each one of us, as individuals and as a group. Only in psychotherapy, where every change is monitored, is it easier to observe. Yet if we can introspect and give the matter careful thought, we are bound to recognize how we ourselves are subject to this archaic mechanism; every step that we take forward is a bid to gain an inch from our basic stone-age self, our primitive mentality.

As we shall see there are forces always working in the mind to preserve the status quo, the existing state of equilibrium. It is part of the tendency of all matter to return to a pre-organic or, in other words, a lifeless state. Consciousness is, after all, a new and daring afterthought in evolution's undertaking. As a heady experiment, it is still hanging in the balance while *homo sapiens* seems uncertain whether he wants to nurture it or to kill the great adventure off. To the universe at large it may not make a lot of difference what happens to these human ants. So it is we who have to choose, to take responsibility whether the species shall

survive or be extinguished by its own hand, deemed to be
omnipotent by virtue of technology.

Why should it prove so difficult for the individual and the
group to take a mental step forward and maintain it
afterwards? There are doubtless countless reasons which
lie beyond our present scope, but one we have already
touched on lies with the concept of the container.

We saw how container and contained symbolize mother
and her infant. In phantasy, that container provides a close
and cosy fit. Experienced in concrete terms, this would
imply that growth and stretching on the part of the contained
will bring about catastrophe, since movement is feared to
represent an attack on the container, which in some instances
will share what amounts to a delusion. Untrue assumptions
of this kind contribute to Laing's notion, the phenomenon
of the 'schizogenic mother'. This, incidentally, is no longer
accepted in those simplistic terms, for we recognize today that
the infant's constitution also plays a central part. The
possessive mother is seen as another version, but a less
malignant one as part of an entire spectrum: containers
which refuse to yield to the growth need of their contents.
Clearly, birth represents one catastrophic precedent. The
memory of that cataclysm lies embedded in the mind as
something which, at any cost, must be avoided in the future.
And for that reason, the unconscious, while part of it is
thrusting forward with a memory residue of original foetal
growth with its inherent satisfactions, if we can apply this word
to a silent, inbuilt process, is at the same time tugging back.
Here lies the nub of every conflict. The difficulty is to know,
with any inner certainty, in countless daily instances, which
argument goes by which name. What are each party's true
credentials: which is Life and which is Death? And how, with
all the smoke of battle, are we to tell the two apart with any
degree of certainty? Which is it of the two opponents that is
confronting us this time? In a given struggle or upheaval which
fills us with anxiety, as every disturbance of the existing

equilibrium will, how are we to differentiate progress from
the stale reaction which will undo prevailing gains?

Just as in physics, Newton pointed to the force of gravity
drawing all things back to earth unless lifted by a counter-
force, Freud saw a force within the mind whose aim is quite
specifically to maintain the status quo or to restore an earlier
one. For this force, he borrowed the name of the Nirvana
Principle. This seducer promises us a perfect state of mind
and therefore, by implication, a perfect state of affairs if only
we leave well alone. It underlies our utopias. We hear it in
the Siren's song on our journeys of discovery and have to tie
ourselves to the mast when we grow weary and afraid and
look for easier solutions than the truth can promise us. This
perfect state of mind is seen as being for ever at the breast,
without a moment of frustration, or going back further still,
attached to the effortless placenta, where nourishment and
oxygen were ours without the smallest effort, even the need
to breathe or suck.

In *Beyond the Pleasure Principle*, written during the First
World War and published in 1920, Freud attributes the
power of the Nirvana Principle to what he called the Death
Instinct. Its activities are secretive and never easy to detect,
for it tends to operate in areas of the deep unconscious,
hidden away in our destructive and our self-destructive
drives. Even in psychotherapy, for all our careful monitoring,
we may be hard put to it in our efforts to get onto its devious
track, its underhand machinations, which are those of the lie
and which sometimes lead to suicide or to other forms of
tragedy that we are helpless to avert with the utmost vigilance,
because we are ourselves corrupted. It is the spanner that gets
into the works of change with the outworn clichés of reaction
which we fail to unmask.

There are areas and situations, most of us can recall,
where we found ourselves conscripted, as paid-up
mercenaries, in the opposition's ranks. For all of us can be
persuaded, because of our dislike of change, that it is to our

own advantage to pursue a certain course, or to maintain things as they are, even if we are very clearly on a pretty slippery slope. We can all think of examples where we were seriously confused in decisions which we took in private or in public life, of instances where we cast our vote or backed facile promises only to find that they undid years or decades of honest toil, where we simply abdicated from true concern and common sense, to find ourselves face to face with the ever mobilized echelons of the Death Instinct, because we have overlooked fundamental signs or guidelines in the realm of human rights, be they our own or those of our neighbour.

We will have some more to say about how we can cultivate the power of discrimination in this field, on which our survival as a species has now clearly come to rest. But meanwhile we must underline that all that favours consciousness with its steady vigilance by virtue of that state of mind also minimises lies, confusion and corruption, and must be on the side of Life. Here we must finally confront a case which the opposition constantly brings against us that we cannot readily refute. It is that our therapeutic stance and our intense preoccupation with charting the unconscious mind have kept us in an ivory tower, in spite of some notable exceptions. That it is by staying there, far removed from the fray to better the social milieu to one in which life affirmation is able to thrive, that we are defaulting in effect to the other side, whether we acknowledge it, or not. Is this argument fair? For here we have 'an opposition' which is really on 'our' side. We should be quite clear on this: that as psychotherapists we are not by any means the only workers in the field of cultivating mental health. Cannot everything we do be undone another time by adverse life conditions?

I saw a girl the other day, an attractive girl, a graduate. When she graduated, she had failed to find herself a job, so she filled the waiting time in with learning Russian as another string to her young and willing bow. Still no job came into sight. Nothing, except interviews, rejections and clocking in to the long queues for the dole, while feeling a burden on her impoverished family. Nothing in her expectations had included this defeat. After something like two years of this sorrowful existence, she started, to her consternation, to hear voices, she explained. Intelligent and sensitive, she was very well aware of the darker implications of this.

'What do the voices say?' I asked.

'They say, "Oh Janie, Janie dear" (this is not her proper name), in a proud, reproachful voice.'

'You reproach yourself,' I said, 'and worse still, you attack yourself for something which is not your fault.'

'But I ought to be able to find a job, if I was any good at all.' Her face was hidden behind her long hair which was a lovely sunflower gold.

From all that has been said before, it is obvious that there is more to her illness than these facts. There must, we know, be early cracks which have widened with the strain of these setbacks in her life. And life will always throw up strains. But society should not multiply our obstacles, rather make provision to cushion us at certain times. We should all be helped to ford precarious crossings in our life: adolescence, parenthood, illness and infirmity and unexpected crisis points.

We often hear the question raised: is the so-called welfare state a sign that we are moving forwards, or is it, as is lately claimed, a degenerate, soft option? We have to be very clear which voice in this dialogue is that of Life and which of Death. There can surely be no doubt that in all its institutions, which are now so cruelly at risk, the welfare state represents a most significant step on the staircase of human progress. We took it after the last war, a nation with a single voice claiming that we were going now to build a better world for everyone, regardless of fresh sacrifice.

This girl stood in urgent need of long-term psychotherapy to avert the approach of a psychotic episode. Her therapy would possibly need to be residential in sheltered housing of some kind, and what is more, for several years. The bill for society to foot would be a rather heavy one. But it is negligible compared to the bill if we default, as it is with every life which falls through the safety net. Lives which are mangled by default are to a society like Beta elements to mind. They can reach a point of no return when, with the best will in the world, nothing can be done with them, just as Beta elements cannot be used for thoughts, or for dreaming, or for memories, but merely clog up mental space. So it is with lives we leave to fester; lives which we do not raise up against mind's force of gravity, ever active to return all things to an earlier state, not only in the individual but in society as well. Where an entire society becomes afflicted in this manner, violent solutions may seem the only remedy, and yet we fail to recognize the violence in such default.

Do we, as psychotherapists, share the guilt of participation in this cycle of default? Or can we claim with any justice that by assisting individuals out of their own slough of despond we make sufficient contribution towards the needed counter-force to stagnation and regression? For it is here, at this point, that we must face the criticism of living in an ivory tower. We can only answer that with heartfelt conviction, individually. No one else can ever know whether we are truly active in the most creative manner of which we may be capable. Those whose talents lead them to the lifestyle of the activist often readily forget that genuine activity enjoys that creative confluence whose flowering will spring from roots of a passionate and serious investment in our inmost selves as the repository of the unlimited resources of our human race.

How can we reassure ourselves concerning our own contribution and whether it has validity on the side of fostering life or whether it rests instead on self-deception, the smugness of mere self-enrichment or a comfortable life? There is no activity which may claim by its nature to belong to one or other side. The priesthood, medicine, the law, the sciences and all the arts, as well as the essential contribution from every other walk in life, can lend themselves to perversion by practitioners who default, who go through the clever motions and reap substantial benefits, make no honest contribution, but are truly sick at heart. True entitlement to the full advantage accrued by honest membership belongs to those who cultivate an examined way of life.

We will sometimes hear it said that Freudian pessimism has continued to prevail, that the human animal is flawed in so many respects that it cannot free itself of hubris and of tragedy, that it cannot make an end of mistaking phantasy for the doing of the deed and may be doomed in consequence to retract the gains it makes. At the same time, Freud defined mental health in basic terms which no one has improved upon. He saw it as the capacity of people to work as well as to love. But what is work and what is love? When all is said and done, are we fated to be doomed to lifelong uncertainty concerning the true nature of our individual contribution? After every working day, from the first to our last, and to our final breath, do we have to stay in doubt whether we served honestly in this well-worn twofold harness to our full ability?

These questions are so awesome we may well despair of tackling them, and yet this is an obligation the human soul cannot escape with each new life and generation, and both break with each dawning day. And so we need to ask ourselves – what is work and what is love? Which is true and which is false, as we view them from the workbench of psychotherapy?

5

Work and Love

In an earlier chapter, 'The Cornerstones of Sanity', we saw how difficult it is in developmental terms to see our 'object' as a whole, to acknowledge, step by step, that we appear destined to love and hate it, both in turn, that we have to come to terms with ambivalence. The sound and fury of this struggle are common knowledge in our day. Parents and teachers recognize that the feelings of the child are often unpredictable. Depth psychologists confirm that through childhood and in adolescence, the growing child blows hot and cold. Adults tend to come prepared for a rather bumpy ride wherever sanity prevails. They dig in and do their best to maintain hope and trust, anticipating better days once those weathers have calmed down and the climate, as a whole, moves towards stability. Meanwhile, they draw comfort from signs that concern for others, as the forerunner of love, and curiosity and passion in pursuit of interests, foreshadowing capacities for genuine, creative work, are more and more in evidence, that everything will turn out right as faithfully believed all along.

But where these signs do not appear, while making due allowance for individual variation, we may need to face the fact that the capacity for close relationship and love has been distorted or arrested with all the consequences that this must imply. For, to a lifelong infant mind, or to one which has regressed, any close relationship offers an alarming threat. In fact it is precisely when a more precarious sufferer makes another bid for love that he will tend to come unstuck in a self-defeating way, which sets a painful pattern up. This pain may gradually lead to abandoning these fraught attempts and to withdrawing further still into total hopelessness and complete abdication. This is when psychiatrists may say the 'case is now burnt out'. For great disturbance must imply that yearnings for relationship are struggling somewhere in the mind to find fulfilment in reality.

In a mental hospital, I occasionally took my lunch to a sunny garden seat. A schizophrenic woman also used this little bench to feed the hospital's stray cats with the remnants of her meal. She would flee at my approach and hover at a certain distance until such time as I had gone. Very possibly she feared that I was going to steal 'her babies'. But I felt that her greatest fear was of finding me attractive and getting all mixed up with me. For two people to come close, both in body and in mind, demands a degree of ego strength. Any success will presuppose that the ego boundaries of both partners are intact to an adequate extent which each party can maintain. For where this is not the case, where the self and the other become readily confused, the wish to fuse or to merge, to use the other to return to complete dependency, will prove of overwhelming strength, while massive projective identification, as we looked at it before, will confuse all issues further, until total chaos reigns.

A confused and fragile person is always hovering on the brink of packing in this shaky self, fraught and frightened as it is, by merging it with any other who happens to come along. On the other hand, he feels terrified of giving up, since this would spell the end of him as a human entity. The conflict rages bitterly, especially at such times as he feels that he is drawn to another, once again fatally, as he will sense. Therefore to remain alone is felt to promise peace of mind, while on the other hand, this is no solution for a member of the human race. This is where the tragedy of the borderline patient lies. And his plight deserves that name. For those healthy beings who take their capacity to live an intimate relationship in every meaning of that word, with its frustrations and its joys, almost for granted, it must seem puzzling that others suffer a lifelong exclusion from this state.

Everyone who is in love will, at moments, throw himself into the experience and the partner with a total plunge and absolute abandonment. But the fragile sufferer shrinks in terror at the thought. How will he 'get out' again? Can he extricate himself? He fears the answer would be, no. Because, to such a candidate for membership of adult love, there is this frightening aspect to any close relationship posing an unsurmountable threat: how to separate again without losing life and self. For his is a possessive love which knows no limits to its needs for gobbling the other up as the infant will in phantasy. Such love is a cannibal belonging to the oral phase; as it is known for that reason that all erotic impulses are related to the mouth. Love like this still means to merge or to eat the other up. To melt for ever and to fuse, never, never more to part – which means to be cut in two.

Since this is the experience of his earliest baby days, which has never been outgrown, any separation brings intensely hostile feelings up. Separation makes him feel positively murderous towards the one who goes away, because this is felt to mean that this other does not care for him, or that he has been driven off by greedy, primitive demands and tyrannical possessiveness. But these murderous feelings have to be buried and denied since the sufferer assumes that they are all-powerful and therefore much too dangerous. He does not realize that the other could survive the onslaught and continue still to care.

Even the strongest among us find parting a tremendous wrench. It tends to be hedged around with the familiar ritual which accompanies farewells, like our nightly childhood ones, sweetened with bedtime stories; or that well known request for just one more, or one last drink. The end of lovemaking can be so painful that we have to fall asleep to awake as two again, instead of two joined into one. To endure our human fate obliges us to accept the status of being separate. Only then can we begin to celebrate our span of life by drawing close in love to others even though separation, death and loss are acknowledged as a part of our reality. As long as we deny this fact, we must beat a retreat in every relationship, sooner or later, certainly.

Those of us who are stronger than the sufferers who deny separation in this way may still have problems of our own. For if we doubt our loving feelings, seeing we have hostile ones whenever separation strikes, or when we see any sign which says the other is, in truth, an entirely separate person, we will endeavour to control that other's movements constantly. For in our anger we will doubt that our loving feelings can suffice to bring that other back to us. Instead of a relationship, we may have a tyranny.

An infant certainly assumes that he controls the mother's breast, its presence and the flow of milk; it is a way of dealing with the sense of utter helplessness and the frustration which he suffers if this phantasy breaks down. Where this actually happens in his earliest infancy where the omnipotent belief that mother as a part of him is somehow ruptured prematurely before he was ready to approach this fateful divide for himself, and in his own good time he will later on control any partner within love to their mutual misery, though less intense relationships may be managed fairly well.

The fetish of the fetishist lends itself to such control. The transvestite *is* mother, meaning the beloved breast. His drag is proof of this delusion. Promiscuity may promise an escape from the fear of loss. Such an individual boasts a supply of lovers, up his sleeve, to keep the dread of loss at bay, and believes he can deny his dependency in this way in the familiar Don Juan role. We often fail to comprehend the underlying panic state, although such understanding may offer little consolation to a deeply wounded partner. These complex matters have their roots deep in the unconscious mind, where these symptoms originate as defensive strategies. In the long run, they induce depression, or may cause the sufferer to turn from close relationships to drugs or alcohol or both.

How are pills supposed to change such personality disorders? Any deeper understanding of the painful issues can only make us shake our heads at the level of denial in which psycho-chemistry is seen as a reasonable solution. This is not to say it has no place as a temporary expedient.

What are pills to offer to those of us whose baby needs were not met in infancy, which were not met sufficiently, or were disrupted in some way owing to illness or to death? Premature loss of any kind may mean that we can fail to reach adult capacity to love. Then any closeness, we assume, will lead us back to all the pain which threw us badly once before and all but devastated us. Why must we run that risk again? So we may love and still hold back. Take a step forward and withdraw. Here is a rhythm of events which comes closer to adult love and still defeats its proper end, that still remains so far away and causes others endless hurt.

In all these patterns we tend to find that like and like associate. A person who has matured in his capacity to love is less likely to get involved with someone on the borderline. But it can happen, now and then, and cause untold unhappiness. Perhaps our disapproval of marriage between Black and White symbolizes deeper fears of a badly-mated pair, in terms of emotional development, since all of us associate Black with Primitive, alas, because our primitive feelings are equated with black or 'bad'.

Until very recently, there prevailed a grim taboo on sexual activity between people who are handicapped. It was disgusting, others claimed. Those who shouted loudest were often handicapped themselves, by deeper failure to grow up. The truth is that we are appalled by manifestations of physical love, which we regard as infantile although the

body has matured in the obvious, outward sense. We know from our own experience, even if it lies repressed, that eating one another up, and 'having sexual intercourse', as we might approve of it, can run each other pretty close. And we are out to punish others for being infants when we fear we are little more ourself. For the achievement of a love which fulfils our highest aspirations can elude us cruelly, when it is easier to attack failure in others than admit it in our self and try again.

But what precisely is this love of which we need not feel ashamed, a love which is not a tyranny, or a form of exploitation, or two babes lost in the wood clinging together for dear life, but a lifelong partnership within whose framework two can grow, together as well as separately? Where loving is to rest secure, in an environment of light and space, where we live and let live, we must feel free to share the whole of us with the other of our choice, who will do the same in turn. We must feel safe to bring all our feelings, of the infant and the child, the adolescent and the adult, into this relationship, and have the totality confirmed without fear of being dropped or rejected in some way – because we know that we will try to take responsibility for this awesome collection to our best ability.

People today may consult sexologists, complaining that their orgasm is not all it ought to be. In this materialistic age when we *have so* many things, an orgasm in one more thing which we feel entitled to. Yet these dismayed men or women may well have little inkling of the state of mind in which true intimacy grows. It may be that they will rarely spend an evening alone together, or enjoy a heart to heart conversation, or a true silence. A total, mutual response, that springs from body, mind or spirit may arise spontaneously in such a range of situations; no one can enumerate them, since many of them will depend on our natural disposition, our capacity for tenderness and openness to loving signals, a sense of living in our bodies, and a full and generous acceptance of our partner's otherness. Such are some ingredients of orgasmic potency, not, as we are often told, technical expertise.

Meditating on this list, we can readily perceive how our capacity for orgasmic interludes, in all their rich variety, is bound to rest on subtle aspects of our personal history, above all our earliest one. Had our parents managed to love us unconditionally, simply because we were their child, the living evidence of their love for one another and for life? How lenient or critical are we now towards ourselves, as imperfect beings? Can we trust and enjoy our many bodily sensations, that inner, tidal sea? Can we afford to make mistakes and even laugh some of them off? Can we do this for the other? Can we recognize our faults and our shortcomings without getting angry with ourselves? Are we Philosophical where our weaker points and lapses from day to day may be concerned?

If our parents were unhappy, can we, ourselves, be different without feeling too much guilt wherever we are better off – happier or more prosperous? If they were happy, can we too, make a good marriage in our turn? What are our inner parents like? Have we finally emerged into our own adult self with enough security to permit these inner parents a good, creative intercourse on which their wellbeing depends, as did our own, in babyhood, when we could not acknowledge this, but felt excluded and therefore enraged?

Our capacity to love will depend on all these factors, but beyond them even more on what we are prepared to do so that we may make our loving grow. Do we expect to work at it, even if this requires thought and, after that, perhaps the help of a psychotherapist? Are we going to stomp through life blaming others for our failure to build a good relationship? Or will we, on the other hand, cut our losses and withdraw and settle for a life alone?

This, of course, does not imply that everyone who lives alone has made the best of a bad job. Sometimes we can lose a love, the very memory of which, may, we feel, last evermore. This could be a parent whom we might idealize through life so that we fail to break the earliest bonds. Many creative individuals fall within this category. Parts of the personality can bypass such a deep arrest and make a contribution which provides fulfilment of one kind, so that one may cut one's losses in other areas, with good grace. Every human life must rest on its own economy and strike a balance in its love-account, based on such alliances as only deeper scrutiny may eventually disclose. Sexuality in love is basically the sum of our life-affirmation linked to a capacity for creative intercourse in many human undertakings. The minute that we limit it to genital activity in the absence of such gifts, all we have is copulation or some perversity. We need to be quite clear on this in the confusion which prevails.

In as far as psychotherapy becomes a love-relationship, a creative intercourse, of a sublimated kind, the deepest obstacles to loving experienced by the sufferer will come into the transference where they can slowly be unravelled, traced back to their origins and gradually modified. How, then, can we expect such a delicate process to run to a fixed schedule, when it will surely unfold in its own span of time? Defences against love and trust, thrown up in our earliest years, must be defined and understood before the task of their dismantling can be tackled, brick by brick. They were erected for a purpose appropriate to their history. Now it must be understood that the original rhyme and reason has stopped applying long ago. We were helpless at the time. Very slowly, we will learn to exchange the role of victim for a newfound mastery in its most creative sense.

Where we did not learn to love at the best possible of times, in our earliest months and years, then learning later we experience some degree of the pain which drove us to evade love then by building those defences up. The same, of course, applies to trust. Once our ability to feel more deeply, be it love and trust, envy or malice, greed or spite and then full circle back to love, with all the turmoil this creates (directed in the here and now at our psychotherapist), once this has taken root and grown, then the hour may be approaching for us to leave the sheltering walls of our second childhood home; not as we did the first time round, when we sneaked or hurtled out in angry, self-defeating ways, nursing grievances or hates, but taking stock lovingly of the inner riches we have gained.

From here on, an ability to love and let love will encounter all the daily obstacles the inner and outer worlds throw up, with the belief that love can win, if not this round, then the next. Out of this affirmation springs an urgency to invest all that is in us readily, without a need for holding back in case we might be disappointed or not receive the right response. To put it in a different way, the previous habit of withdrawing from both the pain and the reward which close, human contact brings will have been modified. For open house of heart and mind is the ground of human love. In this respect, love represents an active state of readiness in which we keep alert and ready for such moments as it comes knocking gently at our door.

Now one of love's expressions is very obviously our work. So what might be the difficulties which keep getting in the way of our contribution there offering us a deep fulfilment, while acknowledging the grim miscarriage of justice that today denies so many the right to work?

An individual who is still fundamentally an infant will resent the need to work. He lives his life by the assumption that he will be provided for. At one extreme, such a sufferer often tends to stay in bed for the best part of the day, to everyone's exasperation; he may convert refusal into symptoms of all kinds, either physical or mental. The message runs: 'I am exempt from responsibilities. I will have to be looked after and, of course, provided for.' There may, of course, be further reasons why such symptoms come along. But 'malingerers' in general tend to be individuals who do not feel capable of meeting the demands of life, who do not trust that they possess inner resources or who fear that if they show them, more and more is going to be asked of them, so .that they may end up exploited. Such attitudes may well be the result of certain ways of growing up, where a child is given signals that only by being sick or helpless will a parent start to show him some attention. Such parents give a strong impression that they are not interested in a baby or child except when he becomes distraught. Only when he is in trouble, when he starts to cry or whine, or coughs and runs a temperature, do they spring into action and show a semblance of concern.

It may be, on the other hand, as is commonly the case, that the next baby came along just as soon as the child could walk, or hold a cup or feed himself. This may then enforce the message that acquiring skills does not pay off. All the reward he got was that he was overnight displaced by the helpless baby, meaning that mother only likes helpless babies she can cuddle and who never answer back.

We do find mothers everywhere to whom this actually applies; but just as often, we meet with groundless complaints and wrong assumptions on the part of a sufferer. Borderline patients, do, we often find, have a mother who cannot stand her child displaying a mind of his own. At the earliest sign that he is separate and acts or thinks for himself, she concludes that he does not love her; if he did, he would be of one mind with her in every respect: docile, passive and submissive. A child treated in this way may, in turn, become a parent of a similar kind.

One such mother became distraught when her son of six or seven began to play with radios. What did he want with all those wires when she used to play with dolls? He was not the least bit like her; he could not love her in that case. What a painful disappointment! 'Where have I gone wrong?' she wept. A child like hers may subsequently not feel free to make a move, since every action on his part may evoke hostility. And since he clearly cannot win, he feels he might as well give up.

Such passivity is not, however, always rooted in parental attitudes. It may be that a sufferer is such a perfectionist that he gives up in despair before he even tries his hand or mind as the case may be; or we find an individual who may live in such terror of his destructive impulses and fears that if he lifts a finger only damage will result, that he is left feeling paralysed. Where fear of having caused destruction is particularly strong, there may be such deep despair of putting matters right again that the inhibition to even make a single move is total, as we sometimes find in the catatonic state of patients in mental hospitals. Only a few decades ago, most so-called 'back' wards would have patients who stood like statues all day long: truly rooted to the ground.

These matters bring us to the question why the ability to work should be so crucial for our wellbeing and mental health and why we tend to ail without it. With work, we make reparation in the outer and the inner world for everything which we destroy both in phantasy and in fact. Why should we speak of reparation for our actual and imagined 'sins', rather than repayment for everything which we have received from others in such abundance, provided that we have been receptive and able to acknowledge it? Certainly, where we are healthy, we recognize that we exist in continuous give and take, in something like a state of balance. Provided that we can enjoy the love and goodness we receive, sincerely and spontaneously, this, in itself, is full repayment. Then our giving, in return, will tend to follow naturally from heartfelt generosity rooted in such happy ground. But where a joyful give and take becomes disturbed at either end, that of infant or of mother, we have a feeling that we rob and plunder others to survive. Then we can simply not believe that anything is freely given or genuinely meant for us. Such are some aspects of repayment. They draw attention to the fact that even thinking in those terms implies that something is awry at the heart of the equation.

Reparation, on the other hand, is a very different story. For from the very start of life we become the victims of our destructive phantasies and deeds, wherever they are acted out. The fear is that our loving feelings may never prove equal to making good the damage done, which urges us to turn to work; work in the sense that it is purposeful and productive, work that has a personal meaning, work that we find satisfying, as opposed to 'the job' which we must take for sheer survival, as little better than a slave. That may sound simple and straightforward, which, as always, it is not. For work, if it is effective in our inner balance sheets, will hinge on our ability to recognize an inner world and mourn our destructive impulses. It is only in this context that work may prove to be remedial in the deepest, personal sense.

Such work bears a distinctive hallmark. It is, by nature, dedicated, seeking no limelight and endowed with deeper, we could say, religious meaning in a wide spiritual sense, because its ultimate concern has to be with restoration of what we feel we have destroyed with infantile omnipotence. In other words it is pursued quietly, with reverence, while it will also not preclude active participation in our intimate and personal life with closer family and friends: even done in isolation it is felt to be communal. Such are the guidelines which will set reparation work apart from something else we could describe as running in circles all day long, while getting nowhere very much, except, perhaps, to empty fame; or to that crass material gain which rests on little more than greed. Here is an activity which is the very opposite from that which has just been described. Noisy, brash, attention-seeking, geared to reward and recognition, all the trappings of success, it merely adds up to a flight from our inmost necessity to repair the damage we have done, and do, because we are imperfect beings who are always falling down even on our best intentions.

In terms of our present language such individuals will be called workaholics. They drive themselves on the assumption that they are indispensable, while their work serves as a pretext to neglect their family and friends, their common social obligations as an ordinary person. Such work is geared to self advancement, promotion and material gain, quite divorced from genuine needs and a sense of true vocation. Its spur is omnipotence, omniscience and the denial of limits and limitations, as well as of our inner world and genuine dependency. It may be rooted in despair that the destruction we have caused may prove to be irreparable, or spring from an unconscious fear that our balance-sheet of give and take has been gravely undermined by an inability to enjoy the good things we receive, very often out of envy for another person's goodness. For envy attacks the qualities in our every benefactor to leave us hungry and in need.

Once again, by describing the black and white of these two extremes, we have oversimplified, for in reality we find that they constitute two poles of what is actually a spectrum, while the values of the culture can easily affect the issue in one or the other way. Today, our competitive, materialistic western culture will generally exert a pull towards the second category. Dedication and devotion, work done in obscurity, tend to be disregarded or, in some instances, attacked as something freakish or obscure. Work as genuine reparation, done with all humility, is readily misunderstood, underpaid and undervalued, as we witness constantly with our nurses and our teachers and others who serve generously, while spectacle and noisy stardom carry disproportionate rewards, beyond the bounds of sanity. But here, as with everything, the eventual outcome may still depend on parental attitudes and the example of prevailing values of our childhood. Were our parents, from the start, generally ready to respond to our earliest undertakings, when we felt these were creative, even if the end result was something like a mudpie? Or did they hardly seem to notice, or even worse, merely scold at the mess made in the process? Were they able to respond to our show of loving feelings? Were they ready to forgive when we were naughty or destructive or were they always critical, creating some drawn-out aftermath of heavy disapproval which hung around the house for days? Did they involve us in their skills and yet not ask too much of us, no more than we were ready for? Could we go at our own pace and even go a short way back if we felt we needed to take a break from going forward in order to consolidate, to catch up with the rest of us? Were we loved for being ourselves, as a totality, or only for our achievements? Were we free to choose our field, even if it was our own and quite unlike that of our parents, or were we pushed in some direction which they thought promised more reward? For it is from this ground, the background of our early years, that our later attitude to work is going to be determined; whether our life's work will vent resentments and grievances, or rise above them to become an expression of our love.

Mistakenly, we set apart certain categories of work which we label as 'creative', generally in the arts. Artists sometimes are creative. Sometimes they are merely clever and pull the wool over our eyes. For this they may reap great rewards, in which case they are closer to crooks, while a carpenter or tea lady, a ward orderly or a fisherman, may be the genuine article. Have we all not sometimes witnessed the most soul-destroying jobs, the most menial and thankless tasks, performed with a graciousness of spirit that makes us feel very small? Genuine creativity is rooted in our inner world. Our works are a manifestation of what is going on inside. Do we have inner objects we experience as creative? Are we able to permit them their creativity with admiration free of envy? Were we in our earliest years able to reach a point when we could finally consent to the parental intercourse instead of attacking it as something which excluded us? In this context, we will find another factor which may prove to be of some significance. Were there, in our childhood background, adults who felt free to share the riches of their inner world with us when we were still children?

There is a very famous painting, 'The Boyhood of Sir Walter Raleigh', which has been reproduced so often that most of us will know of it. The reason hardly lies in its artistic merit; but here is a fisherman instructing a spellbound boy, speaking from his own experience, from his own creative inner world. The painting makes it entirely clear that this is what is going on.

In our society today, children are less and less likely to be exposed to such absorbing ways of learning. Where adults are engaged in shiftwork and children get packed off to school, to huge classes in ugly buildings surrounded by concrete playgrounds and ten foot high wire netting, the chances that their imagination will truly be fired, are comparatively small. And for all the material on the television screen, it will very rarely speak to the individual child as did Walter's fisherman, on the beach, beside his boat. Today we live in a world which is in essence anti-creative. The talent scouts are always out to exploit the latest gimmick in meaningless and showy ways, while genuine creative talent lies as neglected in our time as it did in earlier days, when a Rembrandt or a Millet ended their days in penury. This will always be the case, since genius is the *contained* which threatens to burst the *container* – society at large, the group.

Whether work is loved or hated as a source of joy or drudgery, of a deeper meaning to our life, or something to be avoided at every opportunity, will depend on all these factors and very many more besides. We say that work we love is play. It never ceases to surprise us that we are really paid for it. Why be paid when we should do it happily in any case? True, we need this thing called money, because we have to pay our bills in order to continue working, to have whatever it requires to keep the show on the road of our personal life and tasks.

The endless trash which changes hands in a 'consumer society' is a symptom of 'the job'; the job accepted as a lifeline is a sentence we submit to when our creative resources fail us, in very many instances. If this were not the case, the present widespread unemployment would have met with the resistance which the miners displayed, for their work community is a creative way of life that no other can replace. This is not to deny that where a society is unable to go forward, for a variety of reasons, as is the case with ours today, 'the job' may be all that is on offer, where even this may be denied.

We saw how in love and love's expression, labelled sexuality, all the phases of our life need to find their place and music. How in orgasmic potency in its all embracing meaning, the infant, child and adolescent, together with our adult self, enter into orchestration of this one experience. The same applies to our work if our work is to be fruitful in a true, communal sense. Love and work as states of mind, in their most creative sense, spring from life affirmation at their single, deeper source. And since productivity is linked to creative grace it cannot be cultivated in an isolation of facts and figures, as economists still have to learn.

If we now take it one stage further, what do love plus work add up to, at their truest and their best?

6

A Life of One's Own

Assuming we can reach a stage where work and love become genuine possibilities, what follows on from there along the road we call 'our' life? For we live from day to day and assume life is our own. This, at least, is what we think, if we pause to think at all. But many of us live and die without an opportunity to reflect upon our life expended in the toils and shadows of hour-to-hour exigency, where we can only place our hopes in rebirth or a life hereafter. People may give endless thought to their annual holiday, to a bathroom colour scheme, to the clothes to buy or the right food to eat, its calories or vitamins; they may be busy and preoccupied with such matters endlessly. 'My life is such a rush', they wail. That it in truth is not a life and therefore not even their own, would not as much as cross their mind.

Before she started on her training as a psychoanalyst, or even had an inkling that such an enterprise stood inscribed on the agenda of her life, Marion Milner wrote a book. Its title was A *Life of One's Own* (Milner, 1934). Here she set out to record whatever in each day offered her a sense of joy. Regardless of how unexpected, humble or brief it proved to be, she focused on it faithfully. She then reflected on what meaning this collection, as it grew, embodied for her in her inmost self, and the paths she might pursue. She found she was rewarded with surprises and discoveries which added unexpected facets to her image of herself, deepening and enriching it, slowly, as the search progressed. After further time had passed she was to write another book, *On Not Being Able To Paint*, which grew out of her own artistic struggle. Although she did not know it then, here was a step-by-step progression towards a later epic work: *In The Hands of the Living God*, an inspiring testament and record of her long analysis of a young schizophrenic woman.

We are not left in any doubt that it was the very gifts which she had nurtured in herself, obedient to some inner call, through a span of many years, which she later drew upon to help this insubstantial life lay its first foundations down. For it was partly through her drawings that Mrs Milner's patient struggled to convey the shipwreck nature of her severely splintered self. Deciphering these messages very gradually, demanded all the intuitive skills which Mrs Milner had gathered, as if by foresight, to equip herself for this rescue operation. That she could accomplish it was certainly no accident but the fruition of a habit of personal self-scrutiny, to give a meaning to her life.

Do all of us possess this gift? Do we all 'come trailing clouds of glory', as the great black woman writer, Maya Angelou, said in a television interview? How do we tune into our life, just as Mrs Milner did, to ensure that its roots are nurtured when we know how readily lives can be left to wither or actually be destroyed, although this may not be dictated by lack of opportunities. Then we blame the circumstances. But it is generally ourself who sets about this mutilation although we may not be aware that we are wielding such a blade. We often fail to recognize that we are cutting ourselves off from the mainstream of our life because of our conditioning (social, personal, or both) for various reasons, many of which lie deeply buried and unconscious.

In her book, *Silences* (1980), Tillie Olsen has explored how often writers, at peak flow, seem all of a sudden to dry up. She reminds us how Virginia Woolf named woman as 'the angel of the house', as the one to blame for laying whole generations of good talent to waste in the name of 'duty'. This is true where women writers were concerned, in common with all the other countless wasted women's lives; the compulsion to surrender personal gifts to nurturing other individuals beyond their realistic needs led women time and time again to masochistic self-effacement. This is now so widely known and vociferously lamented that we need not dwell on it. But that men are bound. and crippled by masculine equivalents has been more slow to filter through into popular awareness. For 'bread-winner' and 'provider', as the figurehead nailed to his mast will just as often undercut a man's self-realization and innate creativity, although in less conspicuous ways. For men and women in our day are both still the victims of outmoded images of roles which they are supposed to play at the expense of their own truest nature, only to suffer the extreme frustration and denial of their true selves, a situation which may lead to the divorce court or the lunatic asylum.

The truth is that the more deeply and genuinely we explore the obstacles for either sex to their self-fulfilment as creative members of the human race, the more inevitably we unearth a closely matching parallel for the other sex as well. How can it be otherwise but that the two go hand in hand, although we are not aware of it?

That two waves of feminism followed closely on the heels of war cannot be an accident. We only have to bear in mind how much talent came to grief in the pit of futile wars, where so many men died, or were cruelly mutilated, to recognize that the toll for men has been as heavy, as obscene, and as tyrannical as its feminine counterpart, the deadening life of domesticity, where it is made into a virtue, with all its draining exploitation. Yet while the battle of the sexes rumbles on, while men and women see themselves as two opposing, hostile camps instead of fellow human beings whose yearnings are identical and needs for fulfilment interlocked, how is either to achieve that sense of inner sanctuary from which a true self shall emerge from its embattled hiding place? Perhaps if all of us observed, as did the young Mrs Milner, what momentary situations offer us a sense of joy, collective findings would suggest inner or outer circumstances which make us feel that we are whole: where our existence carries meaning.

If we reflect on this at all, it is a rare experience. Provided we are functional as separate human entities, few of us have quite recovered from the harsh, initial shock that such is truly our condition, that we are destined, one and all, to serve a life sentence which leaves us separate and apart from the substance known as mother. Children whom we call autistic simply do not want to know this. Anything which is not 'me' confronts them with such grief and anguish that the experience is denied. But deep in all of us remains, if to varying degree, some vestige of this total protest. It drives us out into the world in a lifelong search for a solution. One of these is nature-worship: to be part of 'mother nature'. Yet another one is friendship or some wider fellowship, and, above all there is marriage and the relief of parenthood, where we seek refuge in these states as a strategy of denial of our basic separateness, instead of entering into them knowing that we will remain distinct and separate entities for all the closeness and the sharing that we are now committed to by this act of free choice. Instead, we may resort to them to minimize a deeply buried nightmare, a feeling that some essential part of us has got lost or broken off, to leave a wound that never heals.

But certainly to some extent, our primitive and primal being will continue to lament that all these sampled remedies prove more or less disappointing. The wound continues to scream out for better sticking plaster, or some other panacea which offers general oblivion, some kind of anaesthetic that will see us through for life.

Underlying the war between the sexes is our sense of disappointment that even sexual intercourse, however rapturous it may be, leaves us back at square one, returned to this dissatisfaction and at the mercy of our painful wound. Thereupon we blame our partner. 'Men exploit us,' we complain; men grumble, 'she wants everything her way. She's never there just when I want her . . . all this feminism stuff.' What we do not appreciate is that masculine and feminine are aspects of all human nature, that provided we are able to integrate both in ourselves, a creative intercourse within each personality becomes a possibility, to promise a degree of healing from our lifelong sense of loss. This means that if we can achieve mental bisexuality, at any rate, to some degree, our expectations of our partner will become more realistic and gradually less subject to the perennial disappointments that result in hostility.

At this present point in time there is a serious imbalance in our striving for this goal. We have failed to recognize that women are now ahead of the men, in that important respect, in our own society. For women in the western world have by now achieved, even if some of them still fail to recognize this fact, very much wider choices for roles and means of self-expression than the majority of men who have remained trapped in machismo posturing. When I was a young and single woman, some four decades ago, to be seen in all-female company seemed to spell relegation to the scrap-heap of spinsters; a shameful stigma as a relic from earlier times. What a long way we have come, in our own society, privileged as we are, certainly, in this respect! As women have slowly gained the wherewithal for independence, to full responsibility for most aspects of their life, together with the acumen of a penetrating mind, they no longer turn to men to provide these qualities. Those who still hunt men, on these grounds, could be seen as atavistic and still living in a past, a situation which, of course, still persists in many areas of the world.

Today's young women from the most disparate and varied backgrounds are impressive in the way they seem to take hold of their lives in the manner of its subject and have very little time for being the plaything of another, mere objects of another's whim: for a life of immanence as Simone de Beauvoir put it in *The Second Sex.*

Men, on the other hand, continue to lag behind in the task of achieving an androgynous mind, for all the notable exceptions. They still regard tenderness, intuitive inwardness and domestic preoccupations, linked to receptivity in their most creative sense, as rather shameful in a man and the true domain of women, while in their partners they demand these life-sustaining qualities only to devalue them, quite frequently with contempt. There is one reason for this that is not hard to find. Until women had achieved a degree of integration with their masculine principle, they left it safely in their sons by a process of projection; they related to this young male with masochistic self-effacement, bordering on servility. Only when these mothers learnt, painfully, to assemble a more integral mind and achieved more self-respect for their total femininity (riddled with conflict, as it often is) could the sons pay tribute to their mothers as opposite but equal members of the human race, and subsequently begin to shed the burdens of this projection, this extra masculine ballast, to achieve a truer balance as they start to explore their own femininity and the new options which it offers. This suggests that there is now a process under way which will find its own completion in our own society by an inner impetus. As the burden of sexual roles, seen in terms of opposites and fighting factions, is dismantled, the signs are that this will offer all of us a range of prospects to experiment with our lives in a more creative sense, freed from old anxieties that this enrichment spells homosexuality as a blind cul-de-sac.

In other words, provided that individuals have achieved the capacity to work and love, the prospects that they may

then use awareness of this new integration in a fresh, more complete way, as the subject of their lives, moulded to their gifts and needs, seem brighter now than previously at any time in history. This, of course, is not to say that such a possibility, as with each new step that humanity takes, may not appear extremely frightening, seeing that it requires us to learn to make new provisions to contain such growth. Such progress will imply that we are obliged to build new networks of relationship which are genuine and true, and capable of sustaining the force of greater energies which are always liberated by more diversity. Freud's ladies with hysteria illustrated very clearly the quandary of the contained who has no trust in a container and fears it will be blown apart; the more so where the personal bid to go forward is precocious in the individual as the social sense. Then anxieties arise deep in the unconscious that this bid together with the energies it has released can only prove to be destructive. Is there here a parallel since we learnt to split the atom? Is there a terror that we can only put this to destructive use if our social institutions and network of relationships are not genuinely creative in a life-affirming sense? If they, in turn, cannot catch up, to match this release of energy and the new expectations which it raises for wisdom and maturity, for forms of government which rest safely on the self-government of every human individual.

There is a seminal book, written by Garry Zukav, called *The Dancing Wu Li Masters;* it is an overview of the new physics. Here, the author introduces us to quantum mechanics. He explains how the old Newtonian physics, established when Newton discovered gravity, implied pre-dictability. In other words, it stated that 'if such and such is now the case, then such and such must happen next'. But, Zukav goes on to say, 'the mind-expanding discovery of quantum mechanics is that Newtonian physics does not apply to sub-atomic phenomena. In the sub-atomic realm, we cannot know both the position and the momentum of a particle with absolute precision . . . This is Werner Heisenberg's Uncertainty Principle. As incredible as it seems, it has been verified repeatedly by experiment' (Zukav, 1984).

The meaning of 'Wu Li' is 'patterns of organic energy'. If uncertainty applies to the behaviour of the smallest indivisible particle of what we call matter, how much more would this apply to human forms of energy at the most indivisible level of the true, autonomous self? In other words, where individuals, in the true meaning of that word, take up positions and momentum which are intrinsically sane? If the Uncertainty Principle applies to human individuals, once each is integrated and becomes, in that sense, whole and indivisible, then power politics with their obscene manipulations rooted in the death instinct, would quickly lose their stranglehold. Once each is ready to assume full responsibility, as an integrated human unit, meaning the smallest particle, in the widest moral meaning, for his day-today affairs, seeing that they must concern every aspect of his life, as of others whom he loves, and once each of us works together and thereby for others, the individual's response will become 'uncertain' to the politician's aims. It will be uncertain in the sense that the individual is no longer swayed or coerced into becoming a blind instrument for mass destruction of his fellow human beings because orders are issued by some authority above. Approached in such a dazzling light the project of a life of one's own can surely not be viewed as one of idle self-indulgence. Instead, it rises solidly as the bedrock of stability, lapped by creative flux and flow, born of spontaneity which is the essence of true life, as an instinct which is linked indissolubly to sanity.

Could we claim from this vantage point, a century since Freud set out on this mighty undertaking, that humanity has evolved an instinct here for wholeness of the individual with its poignant implications, that can at last be isolated? This momentous possibility had most likely to await our readiness to dismantle the enfeebling projections which theism must demand and withdraw from funds for science as for humanistic progress in each conceivable field. Would it be poetic justice that since the Curies, man and wife, quantified the properties of a new element, which they then called radium, with all that followed on from there, for the death and life of mankind, that in our new laboratory, which is that of the mind, we have begun to isolate the *element of sanity?* To isolate and to describe all its aspects and properties that we might watch over it, as it was earlier given mind to observe the realm of matter. As Paolo Soleri wrote in 1973, 'The bridge between matter and spirit is matter becoming spirit. This flow from the indefinite-infinite into the utterly subtle is the moving arch pouring physical matter into the godliness of conscious and metaphysical energy. This is the context, the place where we must begin anew.'

7

Why Psychotherapy?

How is progress in the cause of sanity to come about once we are clear about its nature?

Psychiatry's answer tends to be, 'leave the problem in our hands. We will *treat* you. We have pills. We have mental institutions, all the fine facilities; we know what is best'. Yet more and more sufferers find an inner deep resistance which can amount to a revulsion from such autocratic trends. In London and the provinces, centres are now growing up which offer psychotherapy. Unlike in a hospital, which is hedged around with protocol, sufferers can come along without a letter from their doctor. They refer themselves to centres in their hundreds every year because they sense they are in trouble. Very often they have been 'under' a psychiatrist not infrequently for years, with a growing desperation, before taking such a step.

In the mid 1940s, when I studied medicine, patients would be 'under' doctors or maybe even 'under' hospitals. Time has blown this phrase away in its more general use. Today some will 'see' the doctor while others will 'consult' him about their stomach or their lungs, the places where the trouble must lie, provided it can be defined.

Not so, however, when it comes to seeing the psychiatrist. Then they still claim to be 'under' him, with all the abject abdication of responsibility such an attitude implies. The phrase means that they have handed over responsibility,

their 'nerves' are 'something' that someone else is going to
'treat'. The word 'nerves' implies the nervous system: the
brain, a spinal cord and nerves as listed in anatomy. The mind
is no longer the central agency. Regardless of the dismay such
an attitude arouses, we must admit that it is one which we
still hold in common, in as far as few of us truly think for
ourselves or act upon the consequences. This is a serious
situation, viewed in the clinical sense, particularly since
'bad nerves' with heart diseases and the cancers are
competing for the first place as fatal illness in our day.

Could they be three different versions of a single malady?
Consumption was once, for instance, a mysterious disease.
But when the causative bacillus was clearly shown by Robert
Koch, it was also recognized by deeper intuitions that the
illness often struck when a person's will to live was somehow
hanging in the balance, or when a deeper wish to die could
be discerned beneath the surface, in many famous instances
which have engrossed biographers.

Today, we can no longer doubt that there must be a
connection between the auto-immune system and the wish
to live or die, at least at an unconscious level. In the latest
scourge called AIDS (acquired immune deficiency syndrome)
a lifestyle has been singled out as one underlying factor. Does
not promiscuity by members of either sex on such a daunting
scale point to a deeper desperation? To lives that have lost
all deeper meaning and that have thereby forfeited the device
for auto-protection built into human nature as long as
mental health prevails, whose deepest instincts are surely for
fidelity and lifelong mating, even though our best intentions
in this direction may fail. Certainly from evidence gleaned
in depth psychology such desperation is confirmed connected
to certain lifestyles. Nor should any of these comments be
read as moralizing but rather as a confluence in a wider life
experience focused on an exploration of the life and death
instincts.

We say how in psychotic thinking or in the psychotic part of the personality, life negation rules supreme, while psychotherapists will find the death instinct at its work in various forms of serious illness, sometimes as a near-addiction to self-destruction in some form. We find that many lives are lived like a game of Russian roulette, on closer scrutiny, at least. What individuals or groups fit into that category? Racing drivers, tight-rope walkers, professional soldiers, steeplejacks . . . where are we to draw the line? Who is dicing with death in a mood of self-destruction, and who engages in these pursuits in a serious frame of mind within a self-examined life? The simple answer is we cannot tell until, in psychotherapy, we find our bearings in the depths where the deeper motives lie. Any one of the above may, in fact, be life-affirming. There is no knowing from outside.

So what precisely are the aims of psychotherapeutic treatment? If we say that we are aiming, for instance, at normality, what do we mean by this expression? Do we see ourselves as 'normal'? And are we trying to influence our patients in our own direction, or some other, possibly? Here we have to be at pains to avoid a dangerous and unwholesome situation where ethical and moral values confuse the issue.

Patients, at the start of treatment, especially those who have a minimum of ego strength, frequently express the fear (if in carefully couched hints) that they will be taken over by this other who seems strong. Once this fear has been expressed and explored from various angles, it will gradually grow clear that such individuals may also long for this to happen. At an unconscious level, they want to be taken in and taken over, as a way of escaping from the struggles of their life and a world that feels so hostile. But it is clearly most important when working with such precarious beings that we are very clear and certain when and where we intervene, and just what we are getting at.

This is a fundamental question which cannot fail to exercise every therapist since Freud, and every prospective patient and his relatives and friends. There must be few professional contracts open to such abuse and on the other hand to such astonishing benefit. Where then, do we draw the line? Where will we make an intervention? What is to be left aside? Freud had made a clear distinction between fear which is based on a perception of true danger and what we call anxiety. Mrs Klein took this further. All anxiety, she thought, as opposed to simple fear, arises fundamentally from psychotic processes. In other words, it always has a delusional basis. Bion then took the issue several steps further still. He recognized that the psychotic uses mental mechanisms to rid himself of all awareness of reality, of the emotions and on from there, of life itself. The same applies to the psychotic parts of the personality even in those individuals whom we would not call psychotic.

Now what would Bion mean by 'life'? Do not psychotic individuals often live to a great age? Are not the chronic, long-stay wards of our mental institutions full of octogenarians? It is likely that he meant a certain *quality* of life which would mirror and reflect a certain quality of mind that keeps open house for the larger flow of life coursing through us as one channel of a mighty riverbed. The more open we can be to this flow and flux of life, this mingling of ideas and feelings, be they ours or those of others, the less resistance we offer, the fewer dams we interpose, the more our life will resemble its intention, possibly. And the healthier we will be.

More and more of us today are frightened of having a coronary, in other words a major blockage in one of the arteries which carries blood to the heart, or of a stroke, which is the same kind of obstruction in the arteries to the brain. Could it be that where we block the free flow of our feelings over long years of our span, that blockage may take on a physical reality? When a patient comes to treatment he cannot, as a rule, express his feelings simply and directly. He hardly knows what they are. He talks of others who are angry, spiteful, envious or aggressive. That he is blocking off these feelings, generated in himself, and projecting them into others, he has, at first, no inkling of.

Doctors, for decades, have told us that coronary disease is due to a variety of causes; we hardly dare enjoy our food these days. In our thousands, we go jogging, frequently with dire results. But cardiologists today seem increasingly uncertain about these forms of prophylaxis. Baffled, they admit the answer seems to lie in the mind, with what they call *stress* and *strain,* in other words with deeper conflicts, all too often rooted in desperate human isolation. If we return to our patients who are projecting all their feelings when we make an intervention in order to interpret that they are in fact splitting off all those negative feelings, which we have listed above, they may at first be horrified because they wanted to be perfect: as all-loving and as pure as the angelic orders. But once the shock starts wearing off and they accept that they are human, they experience great relief. At first, of course, they do not know what that relief is all about. But gradually it dawns on them that as they learn to stop projecting and to take their feelings back, so they begin to feel alive. Very gradually they realize, however painful this may be, that they had, in effect been dead and not even aware of it.

There is an area of deadness, doubtless, within each of us; because of this, we tend to hate and fear the psychotic, who is cut off from the stream of life. This is what Bion meant, that the psychotic individual lives on but without being alive, like some long-extinct volcano. If this is so, it becomes clearer where in psychotherapy we need to make our interventions, that is, when we hear or see or notice anything which is abnormal ('ab-normal' meaning 'away from' the normal). Normality is here defined as fully in the flow of life, in touch with all our deeper feelings and those of others close to us.

Let me illustrate the point. A woman who was very ill, meaning very out of touch, was sitting waiting for her session. The patient I saw before her left in a very tearful state. She

was sobbing bitterly as she passed through the waiting room.
The other patient then came in, settled herself on the couch
and started saying that the paving of her garden was going
well. It all looked nice and organized, tidy and under control
at last. I asked her whether she was paving something over,
here, right now. After a little thought she said, 'Yes. That girl
just now was crying. I felt so sorry but was not sure whether
I was supposed to notice.' A year before she would not
have let herself notice it at all, except at a still deeper level.
Then, perhaps, she might have claimed that she heard some
person say that a course of radiotherapy (hinting psychotherapy) had been known to make one worse, or other
words to that effect, to hide her anxiety that being upset
meant being worse. Sufferers who hate emotions fear that
they are getting worse once their feelings start to drip, then
flow, as does water in a thaw.

Interventions always aim at bringing split-off parts
together and making fragmentation whole. Such a process,
when repeated, over days and months and years will
strengthen a precarious ego and so the whole personality.
An ego which is strong enough can start to sift and sort its
options, assert its true, essential needs to flower into a true
self, which then can suffer pain and joy. A capacity for
suffering will, at last, have been achieved. 'Good' stems from
the root 'gad' – a common Teutonic root – which means
'whole', where 'bad' means 'bits'. In older language we could
say, 'it is a sin to be in bits'. If, then the aim of our interventions in psychotherapy is to bring together bits and help
them grow into a whole, social and moral values will surely
not be our concern. Instead our concern will be exclusively
with understanding.

What is it we must understand? The difference between
Life and Death. If this sounds ridiculous, because we think
it must be easy, it is the very opposite. At any parting of the
ways of, say, two ideologies, or issues in head-on collision,
the ultimate question must remain: where do the pathways

forward lie in this conflicting tangle? How can we ascertain that we are, in truth, not sliding back? People 'have views' but no-one 'knows', *other than the fanatic* who thinks he is omniscient but can, in fact, not tolerate his human uncertainties or share them with his fellow beings in a spirit of trust. Therein lies his deadly power. His is the psychotic terror of our patient in the dark who was earlier described: infantile omnipotence proscribing the sane capacity to tolerate the frustration of waiting in the dark, which is after all one side of the creative process. The rest of us would like to hear many more points of view. We are eager for more information, even if we have to wait. We'd like to check out this or that. We'd like to open the thing up, even if that proves painful, and let the light in from all sides, so as to weigh the issues up. We know that these cogitations are essential preliminaries to *insight* which transcends them all. *Insights actually change us when we are ready to be changed.* Our ultimate contribution to any dialectic process is our willingness to suffer change. Such is the 'under-going' which the fanaticist obstructs by providing ready answers, which by their nature are archaic, and why we cannot afford him. This is why we must beware of such figures in our public life, whatever disguise they come in, since they subvert sanity. Yet again and again in our great democracies we fall into the same old trap of being seduced by 'convictions' when we ought to question them and open obscured issues up, if we are truly to move forward.

A suicide, in many cases, does not really plan to die. Often his intention is deeply delusional: to rid himself of a perpetual sense of inner persecution, something or someone 'bad' inside. He does not wish to suffer change. But the wish for 'getting rid of' is invariably rooted in psychotic proto-thinking. Could we say that we have reached a similar delusional impasse in our fragmented world today? If we survey the global scene, such are our feelings of despair, provided that we have not yet rid ourselves of all our feelings, that we might share a phantasy: blow it up and start again.

We have a precedent to this with the myth of Noah's Ark. Has the time swept round again for this collective phantasy which in the technological age has fewer romantic overtones and amounts to a mass psychosis which is seen in phantasy as so many bunkers while an atomic winter reigns savage and supreme outside? As long as we nurture blind belief in any ideology it carries us in that direction; the dreadful price when we live like so many mindless lemmings. 'Thinking', Hanna Segal wrote in *Psychoanalysis and Freedom of Thought,* 'robs us of the luxury of blind belief'. But to think is not enough. It is only the first step. Our thinking, once the process starts, may point the way towards a pow-wow on the grand traditional scale, one that must today be world-wide, and open up, as we have seen, real possibilities of change. But if it is to be more than sterile, if it is to bear the desired fruit, to be more than posturing for cold political ends, it needs to be infused with feeling and a genuine wish to change ourselves and the world we live in, in the most far-reaching ways.

A major obstacle to this is that our century is surely reeling with the unassimilated impact of decades of mass-destruction on a scale which exceeds our human comprehension. Those of us who have survived and are still in touch with our feelings, agree that we are all but numb. To have actually seen an Auschwitz or a Babi-Yar, a Vietnam or the degradation of a South African, so-called, township, leaves the survivor mutilated. While the media bombard us with news of further holocausts and famines as part and parcel of our daily fare, our finer feelings have no option but to start to atrophy. This process, though we may not know it, has progressed to an extent, where it is possibly approaching the irreversible. This diagnosis must be made without flinching at this time. Our sufferer is now in danger! Where is he to turn for help?

Freud began with hysteria. He found that thoughts, which were not allowed to enter consciousness, were then converted into symptoms. What thought are we not facing now that we have learnt to split the atom? Is it possibly the one that we are now past redemption? Because this is the fear, albeit an unconscious one, of the individual sufferer during his first years of treatment he may not experience remorse. Instead he attacks himself, and then fragments when there is no one, no Self, to feel the dreaded pain. This traps him in a vicious circle responsible for the depression in individual schizophrenics, for *because* he fragments himself, he hates himself exceedingly. Fragmenting may rid him of painful and unwanted feelings, but at the same time he must lose all which is also good and hopeful from inner and from outer sight, and hate himself for doing it, as we are doing collectively at present in collusion with the media. How does the individual sufferer climb out of this lethal trap? By learning with support and help of a psychotherapist to grow strong enough to face his destructive impulses, without resorting to fragmenting, and suffer the resulting pain. The fragmentation can slow down, until it is hopefully phased out, until the personality achieves a sense of being whole. The word 'heal' stems from 'hale', meaning 'whole'. 'To heal' is whole worlds different from what we understand by 'to treat'.

To put our trust in healing means that we have experienced this remarkable process of slowly 'coming together', in other words of integrating the split and fragmented parts of our personality, some time or other at first hand, already, in our living past. Where our own development gets under way well enough, healing has already taken place in deep and fundamental ways. The wounds of losing our placenta and mother-as-a-part-of-me have undergone an in-depth healing, where we are strong enough and well. Where this failed to be the case, psychotherapy may offer a new possibility of healing, even where healing was delayed or achieved improperly, to leave all kinds of festering places.

But if we now move from the individual to the worldwide front, how are we to heal ourselves across the surface of our scorched, blitzed earth, of self-induced fragmentation which multiplies from day to day? How are we to find the strength to grieve and suffer the remorse of the human mass destruction of the holocausts we have caused in this century so we can also *suffer joy* to use the language of Bion, which is essential for survival? When man first travelled to the moon he came back home with a treasure, far greater in its implications than we have yet recognized. It was the image of our earth like a vulnerable blue flower, in an infinity of space. Is it not an image to make the heart drop a beat? Does it not offer us the overwhelming understanding that one false move in the cosmos will make those petals fall apart?

It is common knowledge now that man could bring about a morning when the sun no longer rises. Yet we continue on the path of these deadly preparations, whose fallout is worldwide poverty, war, hopelessness and despair, because we do not want to change, to undergo a transformation in that common heart of hearts. 'Splitting the atom', Einstein mourned, 'changed everything except man's thinking.' If mankind is to survive, that thinking surely needs to change from a rediscovered feeling that sanity and love and life need fostering with all the wealth of the immense resources which we, the guardians of our earth, are squandering so wilfully.

The question which confronts us now is, can we all desist from *treating?* Can we trust that we may heal?

Bibliography

de Beauvoir, S. (1953) *The Second Sex*. London: Penguin, 1977. p. 94.

Bion, W. (1977) *Seven Servants: Four Works*. New York: Jason Aronson.

de Fleury, M. (1900) *Medicine and the Mind*. London: Douney & Co.

Foudraine, J. (1971) *Not Made Of Wood: A Psychiatrist Discovers His Own Profession*. London: Quartet Books.

Freud, A. (1937) *The Ego and the Mechanisms of Defence*. London: Hogarth Press, 1979.

Freud, S. *Complete Psychological Works*, Standard Edition, 24 volumes. London: The Hogarth Press and the Institute of Psycho-Analysis, 1953-73.

Green, H. (1964) *I Never Promised You a Rose Garden*. London: Pan Books, 1986.

Grinberg, L., Sor, D., Tabak de Bianchedi, E. (1975) *Introduction to the Work of Bion: Groups, Knowledge, Psychosis, Thought, Transformations, Psychoanalytic Practice*. Perthshire: Clunie Press.

Grosskurth, P. (1986) *Melanie Klein*. London: Hodder and Stoughton.

Grotstein, J. ed. (1983) *Dare I Disturb the Universe? A Memorial to Wilfred Bion*. London: Maresfield Reprints.

Herman, N. (1985) *My Kleinian Home*. London: Quartet Books.

Jones, E. (1953/7/9) *The Life and Work of Sigmund Freud*, 3 volumes. London: Hogarth Press.

Joseph, B. (1982) 'Addiction to Near Death', *Int. Jnl. Psycho-Analysis* 63 part 4: 451.

Jung, C. (1950) *The Integration of the Personality*. London: Routledge & Kegan Paul.

—— (1950) *The Psychology of the Unconscious*. London: Routledge & Kegan Paul.

—— (1956) 'Symbols of Transformation', *Collected Works* 5. London: Routledge & Kegan Paul.

Klein, M. (1975) *The Writings of Melanie Klein*, 4 Volumes. London: The Hogarth Press and the Institute of Psycho-Analysis.

Laing, R.D. and Esterson, A. (1970) *Sanity, Madness and the Family*. London: Penguin.

Lapage, G. (1964) *Man Against Disease*. London: Abelard-Schuman.

Lynch, J. (1977) *The Broken Heart: The Medical Consequences of Loneliness*. New York: Basic.

Meltzer, D. (1967) *The Psycho-Analytic Process*. London: Heinemann.

—— (1978) *The Kleinian Development*, 3 volumes. Perthshire: Clunie Press.

Milner, M. (1934) *A Life of One's Own*. London: Chatto & Windus.

—— (1969) *The Hands of the Living God: An Account of a Psycho-Analytic Treatment*. London: The Hogarth Press.

O'Brien, S. (1986) *The Negative Scream*. London: Routledge & Kegan Paul.

Rosenfeld, H. (1965) *Psychotic States: A Psychoanalytical Approach*. London: The Hogarth Press.

Searles, H. (1965) *Collected Papers on Schizophrenia and Related Subjects*. London: The Hogarth Press and the Institute of Psycho-Analysis.

Segal, H. (1975) *Introduction to the Work of Melanie Klein*. London: The Hogarth Press, *1978*.

—— (1981) *The Work of Hanna Segal: A Kleinian Approach to Clinical Practice*. New York: Jason Aronson.

Soleri, P. (1973) *The Arcology of Paolo Soleri*. New York: Anchor Books.

Tustin, F. (1986) *Autistic Barriers in Neurotic Patients*. London: Karnac Books.

Webb, M. (1917) *Gone to Earth*. London: Virago, 1979.

Winnicott, D.W. (1965) *The Maturational Processes and the Facilitating Environment*. London: The Hogarth Press.

—— (1980) *Playing and Reality*. London: Penguin.

—— (1978) *Through Paediatrics to Psycho-Analysis*. London: The Hogarth Press.

Zukav, G. *The Dancing Wu Li Masters*. London: Fontana, 1984.

Index

The first edition of
Why Psychotherapy?
was finished in March 1987.

This reprint was typeset using DTP equipment
in Plantin and printed by web-offset
on Tamlux 80gsm Volume 18 paper.

The book was commissioned by Robert M. Young,
copy-edited by Charlotte Greig,
text designed and produced by David Williams
for Free Association Books.